BANK OPERATING CREDIT RISK

*Assessing
and Controlling
Credit Risk
in
Bank Operating Services*

Paul F. Mayland

Bankers Publishing Company
Probus Publishing Company
Chicago, Illinois
Cambridge, England

New Publications Bulletin

Nan, Dan, Beth, and Dave
for their support.

TABLE OF CONTENTS

PREFACE   ix

1   OPERATING CREDIT RISK   1

     Credit Risk   2
     Operational Risk   2
     Fraud Risk   3
     Systemic Risk   3
     Communication Is Key   3
     The Regulators   4
     Cooperative Industry Initiatives   7
     Problems for Smaller Institutions   10

2   CREDIT ADMINISTRATION   13

     The Customer Base   13
     Approval and Review Process   16
     Prudent Risk Management
               versus Aggressive Sales Plans   21
     Thresholds for Approval and Review   21

v

3   STAGES OF EVOLUTION   **25**

Stage I - Informal Control   27
Stage II - Periodic Review   27
Stage III - Interactive Control   29

4   ELECTRONIC FUNDS TRANSFER   **31**

Automated Clearing House Payments   32
ACH Credit Origination   32
Receiving ACH Credits   49
ACH Debit Origination   49
Receiving ACH Debits   66
Wire Transfer   66
Outgoing Wires   69
Incoming Wires   74
Third-Party Access   76

5   CHECK SERVICES   **79**

Check Disbursement   80
Controlled Disbursement   81
Payable through Drafts   95
Correspondent Bank Cash Letters   100
Check Collection   103
Outgoing Cash Letters   116

6   SECURITIES SERVICES   **117**

Receiving Transactions   118
Delivery Transactions   122
Other Exposures   125

7   RISK-BASED PRICING   **129**

Federal Reserve Daylight Overdraft Pricing   129
Payment System Concerns   130
Risk Management Costs   131
Product and Customer Risk Components   132
ACH Credit Origination   133
ACH Cash Concentration   143
Controlled Disbursement   148
Product Profitability   152
Market Acceptance   152

**8   SUMMARY OF THE
RISK MANAGEMENT PROCESS**   **155**

Getting Started   157
Five-Step Approach   158

APPENDIX A   **165**

User's Guide to the Policy Statement
(Federal Reserve Self-Assessment Guide)

APPENDIX B   **169**

Office of the Comptroller of the Currency
Banking Circular 235

APPENDIX C   **179**

Regulation CC
Availability of Funds and Collection of Checks

APPENDIX D   195

Federal Reserve Risk Reduction Policy
Third Party Access

INDEX   197

PREFACE

This book describes a comprehensive package of tools to help banks manage the operating credit risk from electronic funds transfer, check, and securities services. Any bank that offers operating services to its corporate customers will incur credit risk, but many still do not adequately address operating credit risk in their credit policies.

My first motivation for writing on this subject was defensive—as the manager of corporate services at a large money center bank, I needed a clear communication vehicle to support quick decisions by credit officers if a customer's credit quality suddenly started to deteriorate. There was no time to learn the nuances of each alternative in the middle of a "fire drill." We needed a way to jointly respond to problems with speed and confidence. That need, coupled with valuable hindsight, led to the first outlines of the process described here.

In my consulting practice, I continue to modify the process and expand it to guide new customer approvals and periodic review procedures for existing customers. The effort gained currency when both the Federal Reserve and the Office of the Comptroller of the Currency became more forceful in their campaign to reduce payment system risk.

Banks of all sizes can benefit from the tools in this book, but I have found them to be most helpful to banks without a full-time manager dedicated to operating credit risk. The book outlines a proven methodology for assessing a bank's operating credit risk, and it offers cost-effective ways to manage the risk within the context of credit administration procedures already in place.

The methodology integrates policy, procedure, and documentation in a way that forces each interlinking element to be a clear and useful prerequisite to the others. The main elements are:

- Policies that each bank establishes in the context of its own business environment;
- Thresholds for credit approval and review that balance the trade-offs between risk management objectives and sales objectives;
- Risk profiles that describe the mechanics of credit exposure for each product or service, formulas for quantifying risk, and possible risk control options;
- Risk control plans for each product or service that reflect business decisions in the context of corporate policy;
- Regular reports that monitor risk on an ongoing basis;
- Approval forms and worksheets that support the overall process.

Risk-based pricing for corporate operating services is not yet widely practiced in the banking industry, but it is a concept that demands increasing attention. A chapter on risk-based pricing is included to help stimulate discussion.

1

OPERATING CREDIT RISK

With many of the nation's banks still struggling with the consequences of poor credit decisions in the 1980s, there is a strong incentive to look to fee-based operating services to bolster earnings. The most attractive aspect of this strategy is the relatively low call on capital compared to lending. Even with modest profit margins, strong returns on equity and assets can be generated by cash management, custody, and other corporate services.

The irony is that "noncredit" corporate services often entail considerable credit risk—usually referred to as "operating credit risk." Traditionally banks have not fully examined the credit risk consequences of their corporate services strategies. Many credit administration departments do not fully understand operating credit risk, and its management is often left by default to those responsible for service promotion or transaction processing.

One reason credit administrators overlook operating credit risk is the unintentional smoke screen created by other risks that surround corporate services. Definitions of four basic types of risk associated with payments and securities follow.

Credit Risk

Credit risk is the risk of loss due to the financial weakness of the bank's customer. Generally it is the risk that the customer will not be able to provide funds to settle its transactions, usually due to bankruptcy or some other liquidity crisis.

All deposit accounts have the potential for creating credit exposure. The credit decisions associated with depository services fall into three fundamental categories: funds availability, return items, and irrevocable payments.

Funds availability. The decision to make check or electronic deposits available to customers for withdrawal, even though the bank itself may not have final availability in its own clearing account, is a credit decision. This is common practice in the banking industry and is usually driven by competitive pressures.

Return items. The decision not to return checks or reject electronic items presented for payment, even though the customer may not have sufficient funds deposited, is a credit decision.

Irrevocable payments. The decision to initiate an irrevocable payment on behalf of a customer, based on expected funding in the future, is a credit decision.

The exposures that result from these decisions can range from daylight overdrafts of several minutes to exposures that extend over several days.

Operational Risk

Operational risk is the risk of loss due to a failure to perform when executing a customer's transactions. The failure can be the bank's, the customer's or other parties to the transaction including payments networks, communication providers and others. Operational risks include errors, system failures and disruptions caused by natural disasters, employee actions, power failures and the like. There is no necessity for credit expertise to manage operational risk.

Fraud Risk

Fraud risk is the risk of loss due to the illegal actions of the bank's employees, customers, additional parties to a transaction, or outside interlopers. Control of fraud risk is clearly not the responsibility of credit officials, although some fraud control measures do have the side benefit of also limiting credit exposure.

Systemic Risk

Systemic risk arises when a bank participates in a payments or securities clearance network. If a network participant fails to settle and causes other participants who are expecting funds to have liquidity problems or fail in turn, it is possible that a participant doing no business at all with the failed participant could suffer liquidity problems.

   Unlike operational and fraud risk, systemic risk is a legitimate concern of credit administration and credit policy executives. There is a great deal of regulatory concern for systemic risk, and most of the payments, securities and derivatives networks themselves devote a great deal of effort to understanding and controlling systemic risk. Understanding systemic risk requires a thorough analysis of the controls and procedures employed by the network itself as well as a complete analysis of the creditworthiness of all of the network participants. Systemic risk is a serious concern, but it is outside the scope of this book which focuses on customer credit risks.

Communication Is Key

Confusion among risk categories helps explain why credit decisions are sometimes left to operations management by default, especially since controls often overlap risk categories. The process a bank installs to limit credit risk, for instance, may also lessen exposure to fraud. Likewise, operational controls can impact the level of credit exposure. The issue is communication. Better communication is needed between credit administration, the business units responsible for each service, and the calling officers in the field. Senior bank management needs to facilitate better communication by requiring more focused attention on operating credit risk.

The Regulators

The regulators are giving impetus to the drive to upgrade management of operating credit risk. They are clearly concerned that some banks are not devoting enough management attention to the "off balance sheet" risks associated with corporate services, and they are responding with specific requirements that force banks to manage operating credit risk as one of their priorities. The Office of the Comptroller of the Currency and the Federal Reserve are leading the regulatory action.

The Office of the Comptroller of the Currency

In May 1989, the Comptroller of the Currency issued Banking Circular 235 to alert national banks to the risks associated with large value payment systems. BC-235 requires each national bank to periodically assess the risks associated with each system in which it participates, document procedures to perform the assessments, and monitor those risks on an ongoing basis.

The OCC recognizes that these risks are more prevalent in larger banks. "However," according to BC-235, "all national banks participating in payments systems, domestic and international, must assess these risks."

BC-235 goes on to define the risks that should be assessed and managed. They include credit risks as well as settlement/liquidity/systemic risks, operational risks, legal risks, and sovereign risks. The important point here is that there is a specific requirement to address credit risks associated with payments and securities services. The circular defines credit risks to include both sender risk and receiver risk. A definition from BC-235 follows:

> Sender risk is the risk that a depository assumes when it makes an irrevocable payment on behalf of the customer through an extension of credit. Credit can be extended explicitly, by granting a loan, or implicitly, by paying against uncollected or provisional funds or against insufficient balances.
>
> Receiver risk involves risk to an institution upon acceptance of funds from the sender. This may be a customer, another institution, or the payments system. As the receiver of funds, an institution must rely on the sender's ability to settle its obligations at the end of the day. Receiver risk is present when payments are revocable within the system until final settlement.

BC-235 also states the following:

At a minimum, written policies should:

- Require periodic risk assessment of each system in which the bank participates;
- Identify responsibility for assessing risks;
- Document procedures to perform the assessments;
- Require top management approval of participation in selected systems;
- Establish a process to monitor ongoing payments systems risks;
- Require written agreements between the bank and both its customers and the network; and
- Include audit in the review and compliance with these policies.

National banks engaging in cash management, payments, and securities services are bound by these requirements, but the principles expressed in the BC-235 are also appropriate for all financial institutions, including state chartered banks, thrifts, and credit unions.

The Federal Reserve Board

The Federal Reserve Board has been concerned about payment system risk since the mid-1980s. The Federal Reserve Board's payments system risk reduction program addresses systemic risk as well as the direct risk to the Federal Reserve stemming from the daylight overdrafts that banks incur in their reserve accounts when they participate in the Fed's funds transfer and book entry securities network.

Payment system risk proposals. The Federal Reserve Board established a policy of capping the net intraday debits of depository institutions in 1985 and adopted refinements to its policy in 1987. Depository institutions may incur daylight overdrafts in their Federal Reserve accounts up to a maximum cap that is a multiple of the institution's *risk-based capital*. The multiple is based on the institution's self-assessment of its own creditworthiness, credit policies, and operating controls. The cap is applied to total combined overdrafts of Federal Reserve accounts caused by funds transfer and book-entry securities transactions.

A net debit cap multiple is applied for a two-week average as well as a higher cap for a single day.

Net Debit Cap Multiples:

	Two-Week Average	Single Day
High	1.50	2.25
Above Average	1.125	1.875
Average	0.75	0.20
De Minimis	0.20	0.20
Zero	0.0	0.0

Beginning April 14, 1994, the Federal Reserve will begin to assess a fee of 25 basis points at an annual rate against the average daily total daylight overdraft of a depository. There will be a deductible of 10% of qualifying capital, and the fee will be phased in over a three-year period. The Board estimated that, with the deductible, fewer than 300 institutions will be subject to actual payment of a fee.

Self-assessment guide. An institution that wishes to establish a cap category of high, above average, or average must perform a self-assessment of its own creditworthiness, credit policies, and operational controls. The Federal Reserve Board's self-assessment guide is designed to assist institutions in that effort.

Each institution's board of directors is expected to review the self-assessment and determine the appropriate cap category. The process should be conducted at least once in each 12-month period, and the institution must maintain a file for examiner review that includes the supporting analysis and copies of the board of director minutes concerning adoption of the cap category. The institution's examiners will review the contents of the self-assessment file to assure that the institution has applied the guidelines seriously and diligently and that the self-assessment and the underlying analysis are reasonable.

The operational controls that should be examined include the bank's capability to monitor and control its Fedwire position and the bank's ability to monitor and control each customer's position at the bank. Until recently, the focus was on large dollar funds transfer, while controls over securities, ACH, and check services were only addressed very briefly.

The self-assessment guide is being revised to include a broader range of operating services. When the new guide is published, the risks associated with automated clearing house, check, and securities services will have a direct impact on a bank's daylight overdraft cap, above which Federal Reserve fees could be incurred. The analysis of risks covered in Chapters 4 through 6 in this book should directly support the new self-assessment requirements.

Third-party access. The Federal Reserve Board will allow, under certain conditions, arrangements whereby a depository institution or another service provider could initiate Fedwire transfers from the Federal Reserve account of another depository institution. One of the key provisions is that the institution whose account is being charged retains control of the credit granting process by individually approving each transfer or establishing credit limits within which the service provider can act. Another key provision is that the institution's board of directors must approve the specifics of the arrangement.

In addition to the policy specific to Fedwire transfers, the Board is also expected to issue a similar policy with respect to automated clearing house transfers. This is prompted by recent increases in the number of third-party ACH processors, coupled with the growth in ACH volume and the dollar amounts per transaction. The ACH third-party access policy will likely follow the same general structure as the Fedwire policy, the key provision being that the originating depository institution authorize all credits, either directly or under credit origination limits, before the processor sends the payments to the Federal Reserve.

Cooperative Industry Initiatives

There have been a number of cooperative industry initiatives that address payments systems risk and related regulatory concerns. Most noteworthy are the efforts of the Bank Administration Institute, the National Automated Clearing House Association, and the Group of Thirty.

Bank Administration Institute

Bank Administration Institute (BAI) is a not-for-profit professional services organization that offers research, information services, and professional development opportunities to the banking industry. BAI presents information across a wide range of critically important areas, including management and administration; strategic planning; accounting, finance, and control; audit and tax; corporate financial services; consumer financial services; and operations and technology.

BAI's Payments and Securities Systems Risk Project was conceived as a joint industry effort to spread the cost of complying with the OCC's Banking Circular 235. The project participants believed that a joint effort saves both time and money by not duplicating individual bank efforts, especially in the early data collection and risk definition stages of the project. It made little sense to have each bank independently approach the various payments and securities clearance systems in the U.S. and worldwide with the same questions.

A consortium of BAI and 15 major banks completed the domestic phase of the project in 1991. They produced an extensive compilation of information and data on the following U.S. payments and securities systems:

- Federal Reserve Funds Transfer System (Fedwire)
- Clearing House Interbank Payments System (CHIPS)
- Depository Trust Company (DTC)
- Participants Trust Company (PTC)
- National Securities Clearing Corporation (NSCC)
- Fedwire Book-Entry Securities Transfer and Safekeeping System
- Government Securities Clearing Corporation (GSCC)
- Chicago Mercantile Exchange (CME)
- Board of Trade Clearing Corporation (BOTCC)
- The Options Clearing Corporation (OCC)

The second phase of the project was completed in 1992 and expanded the cooperative industry effort to international markets. Twenty-eight separate payments, securities, and derivatives systems were studied in France, Germany, Hong Kong, Japan, and the United Kingdom. Detailed compilations of information and data were produced, along with a generic risk assessment guide to help each bank assess the information gathered in the context of their own business activity. The guide can also be used to structure studies of additional international markets that were covered by the original BAI project.

The strength of the BAI effort was in its analysis of the risk characteristics of the various payments and securities systems. Methodologies for assessing and controlling customer credit risks, which are an important part of BC-235 compliance, were intentionally left to the individual bank participants to address. This book is designed in part to help banks manage those customer credit risks.

National Automated Clearing House Association

While the BAI project helped the banking community by examining the risk categories across a broad range of payments and securities clearance networks, the National Automated Clearing House Association's (NACHA) program to raise awareness of ACH risk is an excellent example of a more specialized cooperative industry effort. NACHA published its *ACH Risk Management Handbook* in 1991.

The ACH network is a nationwide electronic payments system used by more than 15,000 participating financial institutions, 40,000 corporations, and millions of consumers. NACHA was formed as a national umbrella group in 1974 after the successful establishment of four independent regional ACH associations. Forty-one local associations affiliated with NACHA now offer training, publications, and operations support to member depository institutions.

The impressive growth in both transaction and dollar volumes flowing through the ACH network has raised concerns about ACH risk. Risk education is especially important for ACH payments because there is such a rich variety of applications for which the network can be used. Unlike other domestic funds transfer systems, the network is used for both debit and credit transaction types and for both high dollar and low dollar applications.

The New York Clearing House Association has found that less than 0.004% of the individual ACH credit payments they process are greater than $1 million in value, yet they comprise over 67% of the total value of ACH credits processed. If large dollar ACH transactions replace what were previously wires, then overall payment system risk increases, and we will see in Chapter 4 that the credit risk to the originating bank is also much greater. However, if large dollar ACH transactions replace check payments, banks and their corporate customers benefit from reduced risk. It is extremely important that banks understand the risk dynamics of ACH in relation to other payment mechanisms before deciding to implement a new program. NACHA's *ACH Risk Management Handbook* goes a long way toward taking the mystery out of the decision.

Not all of NACHA's cooperative industry efforts are confined to education. It is largely due to NACHA encouragement that the Federal Reserve Board is pressing to convert to an all electronic ACII network. An all electronic ACH will pay dividends in lower risk by reducing the time needed to process return items and by accelerating processing schedules and reducing the duration of bank credit exposures.

Group of Thirty

Another example of a focused cooperative industry effort to reduce risk, including credit risks, is provided by the Group of Thirty (G30). The Group of Thirty is an independent, nonprofit organization established in 1978 to "deepen understanding of international economic and financial issues, to explore the international repercussions of decisions taken in public and private sectors, and to examine the choices available to policy makers." Although the G30 was already well-known for its analysis of a wide range of issues, the G30 has received much more attention since its March 1989 report on "Clearance and Settlement Systems in the World's Securities Markets."

The purpose of the G30 report was to introduce standards for reducing risk and improving the efficiency of securities clearance and settlement systems worldwide. They put forth nine recommendations for consideration by each country, with the most significant being a call for delivery versus payment as standard practice, and rolling settlement within three days of the trade date using same-day funds.

Soon after the report was published, national efforts were initiated to evaluate each major country's systems in relation to the nine recommendations. Status reports from the participating countries were consolidated and distributed in March 1990 at a meeting in London attended by 150 individuals from 33 countries representing banks, brokerage firms, regulatory organizations, and other interested parties. The G30 recommendations continue to have a far-reaching and dramatic impact on practices related to securities clearance and settlement, as each country strives to improve its respective system.

Problems for Smaller Institutions

All of these regulatory concerns and cooperative industry efforts are impressive, and they impact the largest regional and money center banks very directly. But should mid-sized and smaller institutions be concerned with these risks?

The answer is yes—if they are providing operational services to corporations. The regulators insist upon it, and prudent business practice demands it.

The three most significant problems for small and mid-sized institutions are:

- lack of awareness of actual exposure levels;
- determination of the appropriate level of risk control;
- regulatory compliance.

This book directly helps small and mid-sized banks identify and quantify exposure, and it provides them with a logical framework for selecting risk control alternatives. With senior management approval, most banks will be in full regulatory compliance.

2

CREDIT ADMINISTRATION

The fundamental credit administration principles for corporate services are no different than those for lending—the key being "know your customer." Knowing your customer, however, may require unprecedented cooperation in many institutions. Knowledge of the customer's service usage—including transaction volumes and dollar flows—is found in the business unit or operations area responsible for sales and delivery, but knowledge of the customer's creditworthiness lies with the account officer or credit administration.

The Customer Base

There are a few critical aspects that make up credit administration. Some key areas to consider include the customer base, the approval and review process, and thresholds and prudent risk management versus aggressive sales plans.

Consider the overall credit characteristics of the customer base before we examine the credit risk for individual customers. A meaningful overview is provided by a simple graph like the one illustrated in Figure 2-1. The

13

graph plots the number of customers that use a corporate service against the credit grades assigned to those customers. Most banks have credit grading systems with between five and ten categories of obligor risk. A credit grading system with nine categories of risk is used in this chapter for the purpose of illustration.

1 - Relative absence of credit risk
2 - Minimal credit risk
3 - Average credit risk
4 - Acceptable with more than average credit risk
5 - Less than acceptable credit risk
6 - Excessive credit risk—performing as agreed
7 - Excessive credit risk—nonperforming
8 - Potential loss—doubtful
9 - Uncollectible

The overview in Figure 2-1 is a prerequisite to designing an effective credit administration process for corporate services, and the fact that the

Figure 2-1   Credit Grade Distribution

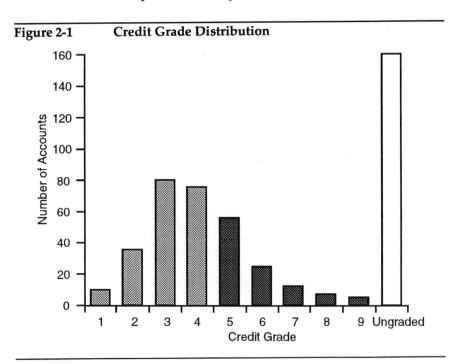

data is difficult to obtain for many banks explains a lot about the practical problems of managing operating credit risk. Most banks do not have the internal systems in place to readily match service product data with credit grade data. Nevertheless, the task can be accomplished by designing a simple stand-alone program and feeding it with data extracted separately from credit and transaction processing systems. Many banks have an "information center" or other ad hoc reporting capability to match extracts from unrelated systems.

The distribution of grades in Figure 2-1 is typical of what might be found for any given service or product. Note that in this case there is a very large number of ungraded (nonborrowing) customers. The number of non-borrowing customers who use certain services can be very large. A typical example is direct deposit of payroll, which is often sold through the branch system as an adjunct to an operating account. Many times the customer does not have a borrowing relationship with the bank, and the service is often sold to the customer by a third-party payroll processor.

Other services are more relationship oriented and have few ungraded or nonborrowing customers. Deposit concentration, a service where each day the bank sweeps local deposits from multiple banks into one central concentration account, is an example of a relationship oriented service. The bank often has a borrowing relationship with deposit concentration customers, so a large number of ungraded customers would be less likely than for direct deposit.

Figure 2-1 shows that there are two main concerns that need to be investigated and managed: that portion of the customer base with known poor credit quality; and that portion of the customer base which is ungraded and the credit quality is unknown.

The number of customers falling into these two categories is very important, but the actual dollar exposure is even more meaningful. Figure 2-2 overlays the dollar exposures on the same graph as the one indicating the number of customers in each credit grade. In this illustration, the dollar exposures in the poor and ungraded categories are disproportionately larger than the number of customers. The problem is especially pronounced in credit grade of seven, where one customer is apparently a very large user of the service.

Periodic snapshots like this can indicate to management and the auditors whether operating credit risk is a serious concern, and whether the bank's approval process for new customers and periodic review of existing customers should be tightened or revised.

Figure 2-2   **Comparison of Dollar Exposure Versus**
                    Number of Accounts

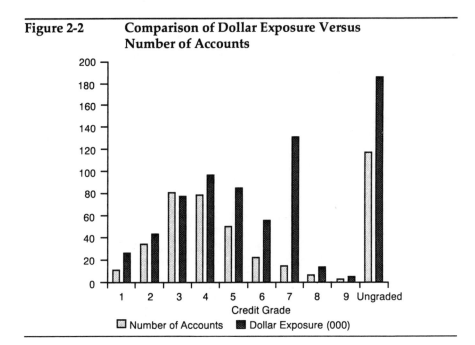

Credit Grade

☐ Number of Accounts   ■ Dollar Exposure (000)

Approval and Review Process

How involved in the approval and review process does credit administration need to be? To a very large extent, the answer depends upon the individual institution, its credit policies, and the aggressiveness of its sales plans for corporate services. This can be illustrated by presenting a sample review and approval process and then looking at alternative approaches with their corresponding rationales.

The sample process that follows illustrates one of the many possible ways to approve and review operating credit risk. In this case, the bank uses the nine category credit grading system described previously, and the bank's credit policy mandates that officers with lending authority approve operating credit risk.

The sample process is divided into sections for new customer approval and periodic review of existing customers.

Sample Approval and Review Process

1) *New Customer Approvals*

   a) *Credit grades 1-4*
   Customers with good credit grades are approved in the same manner as loans. *The account officer approves the maximum exposure expected for the service under normal unsecured lending authority.* See Figure 2-3 for a sample approval form and refer to Chapter 8 for more information.

   Note the specific instructions on the form requiring the active use of product credit risk profiles.

   The account officer is responsible for estimating the expected exposure based on discussions with the customer regarding the objectives and expected volumes for the service to be approved. The calculation depends on the specific service requested and is described in Chapters 4 through 6.

   b) *Credit grade 5*
   Watch list customers require a second more senior credit approval in addition to the account officer. Chapters 4 through 6 describe action steps for deteriorating credits, and these additional measures should be seriously considered before approving grade 5 customers for the service. In some cases, the action steps can totally eliminate the credit exposure. The important point in this example is that the approval decision is clearly left to senior credit authorities.

   c) *Credit grades 6-9*
   The service is not offered to customers with extremely poor credit grades without requiring action steps that eliminate or dramatically reduce the exposure. Many banks will not approve additional services under any circumstances as a matter of policy. Others see a benefit in improved information and control for a bank if the transactions of borrowing customers with severe financial difficulty flow through the bank.

   d) *Ungraded customers*
   The account officer is responsible for calculating the maximum expected exposure for all nonborrowing customers who request operating services.

   If the exposure is less than $50,000 the account officer approves the service under normal unsecured lending authority.

   If the maximum expected exposure is greater than $50,000, the account officer requests that the customer be credit graded and procedures for credit graded customers are followed.

2)   *Periodic Review of Existing Customers*

   a) *Credit grades 1-4*
       The account officer includes the credit risk from operating services in the annual review. In this example, the bank categorizes the risk inherent in each service as high, medium, or low. For high and medium risk services, a history of dollar exposures is required for the annual review. For low risk services, to reduce the volume of reporting required to support the annual review, dollar histories are not required.

   b) *Credit grades 5 or worse*
       The account officer is required to track all operating services the customer uses on a monthly basis. Operating departments generate monthly reports of transaction and dollar volumes for each service that watch list customers use.
       The account officer determines if the maximum approved exposure was exceeded and if the action steps for deteriorating credits should be applied or tightened.

   c) *Ungraded customers*
       All nonborrowing customers with unknown credit quality should be reviewed periodically by credit officials for maximum credit exposure. To reduce the work load to a practical level, the bank in this example requires the account officer to formally review only those nonborrowing customers who use operating services rated high in credit risk.
       The account officer continues to be responsible for "knowing the customer" and the exposure created by medium and low risk services.
       If the maximum exposure occurrence exceeds $50,000, the account officer is responsible for requesting credit grading and following the review procedure for graded customers.

3)   *Deteriorating Credits*

   Customers who are downgraded between periodic reviews receive immediate attention. The account officer and a second more senior credit official are required to immediately determine if any action steps are needed to reduce or eliminate exposure.

   The approval and review process in this example is summarized in flowchart form in Figure 2-4. The chart lends itself to a focused discussion of the bank's specific decision thresholds, and it allows easy comparison with alternative ways to manage operating credit risk.

**Figure 2-3   Sample Approval Form
                    Cash Management Credit Exposure**

Customer Name   _____

Customer Number   _____

Product

High Credit Risk:	Medium Credit Risk:	Low Credit Risk:
❐ ACH	❐ Wire Transfer	❐ Lock Box
❐ Depository Transfer Checks	❐ Zero Balance Accounts	❐ Other _____
❐ Other _____	❐ Controlled Disbursement	
	❐ Payable Through Drafts	
	❐ Other _____	

Maximum Expected Exposure

$ _____

Customer Credit Grade

❐ Grade _____   ❐ Ungraded

Risk Reduction Measures

_____
_____
_____
_____

Approvals

a. Customer with credit grade 1 - 4 requires account officer approval.
b. Customer with credit grade 5 requires senior approval after consideration of risk reduction measures.
c. Customer with credit grade 6 - 9 requires risk reduction measures and senior approval.
d. Ungraded customer with less than $50,000 maximum expected exposure requires account officer approval.
e. Ungraded customer with $50,000 or more maximum expected exposure requires credit grading before approval.

Approved: _____

Approved: _____

Figure 2-4   Example 1: Thresholds

New Approval

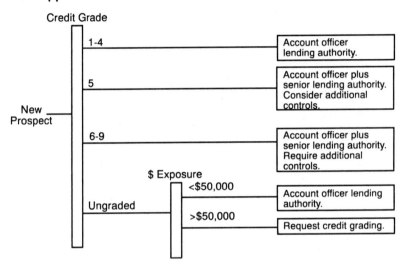

Periodic Review

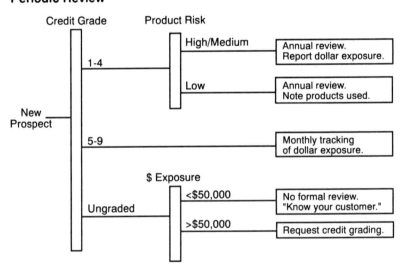

Prudent Risk Management versus Aggressive Sales Plans

A key question in many banks concerned with operating credit risk is: how can prudent risk management be *balanced* with aggressive sales plans to support strategic revenue goals? Some business unit managers view credit concerns as an overplayed obstacle to their sales effort. They argue that historic loss rates are low and that a process similar to Figure 2-4 is unnecessary and counterproductive. Some claim that through their own operating procedures they have reduced operating credit risk to levels that make credit administration oversight unnecessary.

Chapters 4 through 6 show that operating procedures and product features can indeed impact the level of operating credit risk. In some cases, business unit managers can legitimately claim to have removed the credit risk. The alternatives for approval and review need to be analyzed by each bank on a product by product basis.

In all cases, the final decision as to the best way to manage operating credit risk should be made by senior management. Both the principles of prudent management and the specific requirements of the regulators make this mandatory.

Thresholds for Approval and Review

One way to moderate the impact of credit administration procedures on a sales oriented business is to change the thresholds for action—if the impact of the changes is tested and justified by a thorough analysis of the data.

Modified Thresholds

Figure 2-5 uses the same basic structure as the first example in that the first threshold each new approval must pass through is credit grade, but it is pared down to two instead of three credit grade groupings. The new example also relaxes the exposure threshold for ungraded customers to $75,000 from $50,000 before credit grading becomes mandatory. Both of these threshold modifications have the effect of reducing the bureaucratic and psychological obstacles to an aggressive sales program. With appropriate analysis of the number of potential customers and dollars that are impacted by alternative thresholds, the right balance can be found.

Figure 2-5   Example 2: Thresholds

New Approval

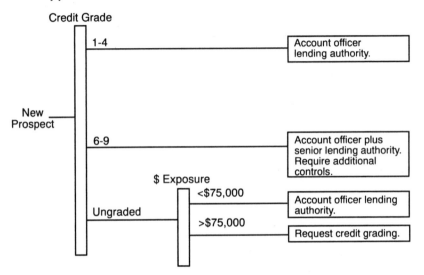

Periodic Review

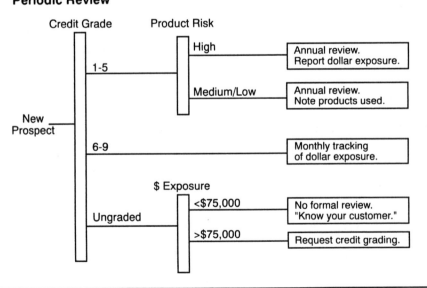

The same principle applies to periodic review of the existing customer base. Again, in both examples the primary filter is credit grade. High graded customers pass through a product risk filter that reduces the review effort, and ungraded customers pass through a dollar exposure filter. Figure 2-5 loosens the credit grade, product risk, and dollar exposure criteria.

New Structure

An alternative is to use an entirely different sequence of thresholds. Instead of the structure in Figure 2-5, which is primarily credit grade driven, the third example in Figure 2-6 is driven by product type and exposure level. Both approaches can work well, as can other threshold sequences. The strength of the product driven approach is that the business unit responsible for the service can often eliminate the need for customer credit approval because it has the option of building product features that limit risk.

There are many ways to control operating credit risk to the satisfaction of senior management and the regulators, but in all cases, the risks must be identified and measured on a regular basis, control procedures must be well documented, and responsibility for risk management must be clearly assigned.

Figure 2-6   Example 3: Thresholds

New Approval

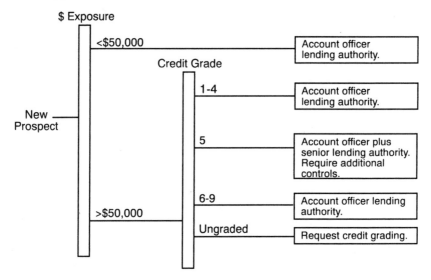

Periodic Review

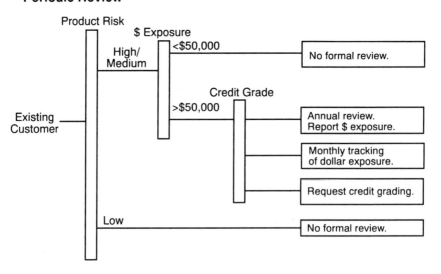

3

STAGES OF EVOLUTION

The diversity of product types that cause credit risk, and the variety of control options available for each product, can make the control of operating credit risk seem unduly complicated. In fact, most banks are well positioned to make the necessary decisions because the risk taking infrastructure is already there. Credit risk is an integral part of banking.

Because of the variety of choices, there are no absolutely right or wrong ways to manage operating credit risk. A bank's process for managing operating credit risk should evolve gradually as its operating businesses grow, and the pace of evolution should be determined by management's analysis of the business trade-offs between the costs and benefits of risk control.

This chapter outlines the three main stages of risk control evolution: informal control, periodic review, and interactive control. Figure 3-1 summarizes the main characteristics of each stage. The stages provide an overall perspective of the key elements of operating credit risk and they lead to the basic control approaches that can be employed. The management challenge is to determine which stage is most appropriate from both a business and regulatory perspective.

The results of management's analysis are likely to vary by product. The control process in the previous chapter suggested that different products offered by a bank could require different levels of control. "High risk" products required more stringent risk control than "low risk" products.

Figure 3–1   Stages of Evolution

Stage I Informal Control	Stage II Periodic Review	Stage III Interactive Control
1. Little attention is given to operating credit risk at senior levels. 2. No formal integration of operating credit risk into credit administration process. 3. Little specific knowledge of operating credit risk by credit authorities. 4. Operating areas can make credit decisions by default.	1. Customers are pre approved, but actual credit risk is reported *after* it occurs. 2. Limited integration of operating credit risk management into the credit administration process. 3. Changes in exposure levels may be unknown to credit authorities between reviews. 4. Policies and procedures are adjusted periodically by credit authorities.	1. Exposure is prevented *before* it occurs. 2. Full integration of operating credit risk into the credit administration process. 3. Processing systems block transactions and require credit approval if credit limits are exceeded. 4. Credit limits are changed as customer credit grades and volumes change.

Stage I - Informal Control

In Stage I, there is little attention to operating credit risk at senior levels. There is no formal integration of operating credit risk into the credit administration process, and there is little specific knowledge of operating credit risk by credit authorities.

If the bank does little or no operating business, this lack of management attention may be entirely appropriate. On the other hand, if significant exposures do exist, it is vital that proper controls are installed immediately. The most important management responsibility in Stage I is to confirm that operating credit risk is not a problem. In other words, is the bank appropriately in Stage I by design, or is it in Stage I through lack of attention?

The most significant characteristic of Stage I is that operating areas may be making credit decisions—either knowingly or unknowingly. They may be making credit decisions by default because the bank does not have a process in place to make operating credit decisions. The important point is this: If the bank offers operating services that do create credit risk, and a formal process for controlling operating credit risk is not in place, then operating areas *are* making credit decisions.

All banks in Stage I need to formally identify their potential exposures, quantify any actual risk, and establish appropriate policies and procedures as necessary. Education is key to this process because credit authorities in Stage I have very little specific knowledge of the exposures that exist or the mechanics of how they arise. Chapters 4 through 6 can be very useful in the education effort because they describe specific product exposures. They also provide worksheets to help quantify and assess each product exposure.

If after education and risk assessment, it is determined that policies and procedures are required for operating credit risk, they usually lead to Stage II—periodic review by credit authorities.

Stage II - Periodic Review

The approval and review process that was used as an example in the last chapter is typical of the kinds of control employed by banks in Stage II. There are two very important characteristics of the periodic review stage that distinguish it from the informal controls typical of Stage I.

First, a formal process is established in Stage II for periodically reviewing the credit exposure of each existing customer. The frequency of the review usually depends upon both the credit grade of the customer and the riskiness of the products the customer uses. A related process is also established to monitor overall exposure created by each operating product. Figure 2-2, which looks at product exposure by credit grade, is a good example of the information that should be examined. Chapters 4 through 6 suggest numerous report formats that are based upon the specific risk characteristics of each service reviewed. The purpose of the reports is twofold: to enable management to detect changes in credit exposure; and to document absolute exposure levels. Besides indicating to management whether additional actions are required to control operating credit risk—either for a specific customer or a specific product—periodic review ensures that there is adequate communication and coordination among the credit administration department, the business unit responsible for the service, and the account officer or specialist responsible for the sale.

The second major characteristic that distinguishes Stage II from Stage I is the formal credit approval process that is established in Stage II for new corporate customers. The process is usually tailored to specific services. Potential customers must meet certain criteria, established by credit policy, before they are allowed to use designated products.

Tensions often develop between credit officials and the units within the bank which are responsible for product sales. Those tensions are usually mitigated over time with a well-designed approval process. The approval process must be justified by a thorough analysis of the data and it must include ongoing education that describes its rationale regarding the specific product risks involved. Agreement and consensus on the proper setting of each threshold for action that was discussed in the last chapter is extremely important to the overall success of the Stage II risk management process.

Although periodic review provides a great deal more control than Stage I, it is important to remember that in Stage II, operating credit exposures are reported to credit authorities after the exposure has already occurred. Changes in exposure levels may be unknown to credit authorities between reviews, and more importantly, there is no mechanism in place to prevent unwanted exposure occurrences that would not have been approved in advance. Therefore, even though credit authorities have a very important role to play in the periodic review program, the control they exercise is still somewhat limited.

Nevertheless, most banks who offer operating services to their corporate customers employ Stage II controls for most products with credit risk, and for the vast majority of banks, Stage II controls are fully adequate. Based on management's periodic review, policies can be modified and adjustments can be made as needed to specific approval thresholds.

Stage III - Interactive Control

Interactive controls are more expensive than periodic review, and consequently they are usually applied by most banks on a very selective basis only. The main characteristic of interactive control is that it prevents exposures before they occur. With interactive control, credit authorities not only have the ability to establish exposure limits for each customer, but the transaction processing system is programmed to block any transactions that exceed a given customer's limit. The customer's blocked transactions are not released for execution until the overlimit situation has been referred to a designated credit officer with the authority to approve or reject the overlimit transactions.

The best example of interactive control is the capability many banks have installed to prevent their customers from creating a daylight overdraft when they instruct the bank to initiate an outgoing wire transfer before they have sufficient available balances on deposit. To prevent this from happening, many banks have their wire room check the intraday balance for sufficient funds before a wire is released. Some banks will facilitate the process for creditworthy customers by establishing intraday lines of credit. If the balance is insufficient, or if a credit line has not been established to cover the shortfall, the account officer must be contacted for approval before the wire can be released.

In reality, there are very few banks that currently employ interactive controls for services other than wire transfer. This is likely to change rapidly for many banks, however. With the rapid growth of ACH transaction and dollar volumes, coupled with the increasing publicity regarding ACH risk, ACH is the next most likely candidate. Most banks who offer ACH services to their corporate clients are actively examining the need for better risk control, and some are now beginning to install Stage III interactive controls for ACH. Chapters 4 through 6 identify each of the interactive control options that are feasible for the ACH products examined, as well as other products as appropriate. The examination of these additional control options for each product helps support the objective of providing management with a broad perspective on the key elements of operating credit risk and the control approaches that can be employed.

The obvious constraint on banks that are considering the use of interactive controls for a broader range of their operating products is cost. The two main cost considerations are software enhancements and a practical credit referral process.

For most banks, the major cost of interactive control is the expense involved in developing or purchasing software so their processing systems can block the transactions that create overlimit situations for specific customers. Although this is a significant obstacle, software costs will come down as demand for interactive control increases. For instance, most wire transfer software packages are now designed with interfaces to allow for balance checking and overlimit blocks, and an increasing number of ACH software vendors are now providing risk modules with similar blocking capabilities. In a very short time, interactive control features will be standard for most ACH software.

The other significant cost obstacle is the referral system, whether the bank decides to approach it on a manual or automated basis. One of the problems associated with gaining credit approval for specific transactions is the tight timing needed for a decision. The approval is often required during evening hours, and in the case of ACH, there are often tight daily processing deadlines in the evening.

When banks find that the customer's regular account officer is unavailable in the evening, some have found it necessary to assign "duty officers" to handle credit decisions during off hours. The benefit is that the duty officer can be highly knowledgeable regarding product issues, but may be less likely to understand the credit nuances of the specific customer. Nevertheless, referral problems created by interactive controls for an increasing array of products can often be handled by piggybacking on a system that already exists—most likely to approve the exposures caused by daylight overdrafts due to wire transfers.

Each bank has to make its own business decision regarding interactive controls by weighing current and expected exposures against the additional cost of interactive control. The following chapters provide a comprehensive methodology for assessing and monitoring the information that each bank needs to evaluate its need for increased levels of risk control.

4

ELECTRONIC FUNDS TRANSFER

The electronic funds transfer (EFT) services include consumer and corporate automated clearing house (ACH) payments; financial electronic data interchange (EDI), which often uses the ACH network; and wire transfer services that use both the Fedwire and Clearing House Interbank Payments System (CHIPS) networks.

According to the National Automated Clearing House Association (NACHA), the average dollar value of a single payment in 1991 was:

CHIPS	$5,210,958
Fedwire	3,043,333
ACH	3,832
Check	1,336

The total annual dollar value processed by each payment system in 1991 was:

Wire transfer	$421 trillion
Check	60 trillion
ACH	6.9 trillion

These aggregate dollar amounts help put an overall industry perspective on sources of risk, but it is important for each individual bank to assess its own risks associated with each service it offers to its corporate customers. Individual banks should consider both the magnitude and duration of their exposure as well as the factors that impact the likelihood that they will suffer a loss. Obviously the particular controls a given bank employs will impact the assessment greatly. Even if there are more dollars flowing through a service offered by a bank using Stage III interactive controls than flowing through a bank using Stage II periodic review, the Stage III bank probably has less risk.

Automated Clearing House Payments

The ACH was created in the early 1970s as an electronic substitute for the ever growing volume of checks processed by the banking system. It was designed as a low cost, high volume, batch processed system with settlement several days in the future.

ACH is unique among the payment systems in that it encompasses both credit and debit transactions. An ACH debit is similar to a check in that it flows from the payee originator to debit the account of the payor receiver. An ACH credit is similar to a wire transfer in that it flows from the payor originator to the payee receiver (Figure 4-1).

Some bankers are concerned that the relatively low price of ACH transactions could encourage high dollar wire transfers to switch to the ACH, adding risk to the overall payments system. The advent of EDI payment formats in the mid-1980s highlights the problem, since it encourages using the ACH for high dollar payments.

In reality, the ACH is a multipurpose payments system that can efficiently handle a variety of debit and credit-based products for both low and high dollar applications.

ACH Credit Origination

There is a wide and growing variety of services that banks can offer their corporate customers based upon the ACH network. Typical ACH credit services include both consumer and corporate transactions.

Figure 4-1   Comparison of Payment Methods

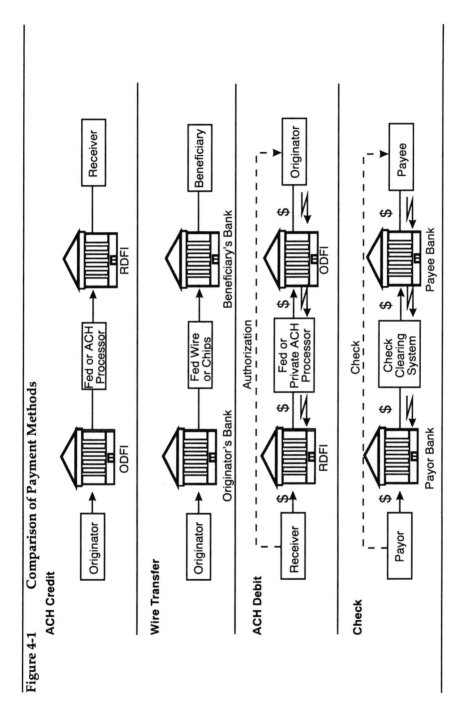

Consumer transactions are generally for relatively small dollar amounts, and they include:

- direct deposit of payroll, pensions and annuities;
- dividend payments;
- telephone bill paying by consumers.

Examples of large dollar corporate transactions include:

- financial EDI for corporate vendor payments;
- electronic tax payments;
- account replenishment services (e.g., periodically funding local payroll disbursement accounts from a central corporate account).

Consumer Example – Direct Deposit of Payroll

Direct deposit of payroll services enable companies to deposit employee pay directly into individual checking, savings, or money market accounts at financial institutions throughout the country. The service provides for the electronic transfer of funds from the company's corporate demand deposit account to employee accounts using ACH credits.

Several days prior to the payday, the company transmits an electronic file of payment orders to its bank with the net amount to be credited to each employee, along with the appropriate payment dates, routing numbers, and account numbers. Some banks also accept physical delivery of magnetic tapes or diskettes. After extracting "on-us" items, the bank delivers the payment file to the ACH processor. The credit transactions then move through the ACH network and are credited by the receiving financial institutions to each employee account on payday.

Corporate Example – Financial EDI

ACH/EDI corporate disbursement services offer a bank's corporate customers an electronic alternative to using checks for corporate-to-corporate payments. EDI services include the movement of remittance data along with the movement of the actual dollar payments. Remittance data can be delivered through the ACH payment network by using addenda records specifically designed for that purpose, or it can be delivered directly by the bank, a "value added network," or another third party service provider. Financial EDI is usually viewed as a subset of a much broader EDI program that a growing number of corporations are pursuing in an effort to improve their efficiency, customer service, and competitiveness.

For the typical EDI service, a file of payment orders and accompanying remittance data is transmitted by the corporation to its bank, usually in a standard EDI format developed by ANSI (American National Standards Institute) or EDIFACT (the international EDI standard) or NACHA. The bank will then, in turn, deliver the payments to each payee or supplier account at banks throughout the country using the ACH network. Many banks will convert their customers' EDI formatted payment orders to NACHA payment formats as part of the service.

The remittance data can be delivered to the supplier's bank with the payment for subsequent delivery to the supplier, or it can be delivered directly by the originating bank or value added network to the supplier. The electronic remittance data enables the supplier to automatically update its accounts receivable system with minimal manual intervention.

Credit Risk Description

There are many other examples of the way the ACH network is used by banks to offer corporate services, but regardless of the specific application, the mechanics of ACH credit risk is the same.

According to NACHA rules, the originating bank guarantees payment when it releases entries to the ACH processor—either the Federal Reserve or a private processor. This generally occurs one or two days prior to the payment date. Most banks require their corporate customers to fund their disbursement accounts by the payment date, not several days earlier when the bank releases entries to the ACH processor. The bank's account at the Federal Reserve is debited on the payment date, regardless of whether the company funded its disbursement account. The result is that the bank has in effect extended credit to its corporate customer from the time it released the credit entries to the ACH processor until it is funded by the customer on the payment date.

A company with liquidity problems could fail to fund the disbursement account or declare bankruptcy. If the bank has already released the payment entries to the ACH processor, NACHA rules preclude recalling or reversing the payment entries, even if the disbursement account is unfunded. The sequence of events that creates this credit risk is outlined in Figure 4-2.

Figure 4-2   ACH Credit Origination

DAY 0	DAY 1	DAY 2
ACH credit file is sent by company to the bank directly or via third party vendor.	ACH credits are delivered to the local banks by the ACH processor.	The bank expects funding by the company.
The bank processes file and delivers transactions to the ACH processor.	Customer declares bankruptcy.	The bank's Federal Reserve account is debited.
Entries are effective on Day 2.		The bank has an unsecured claim against the company for the entire amount of the ACH credit file if funding does not occur.
	Bank Exposure	

Source: NACHA

Customer Risk Calculation

The maximum exposure a bank has to a corporate customer that originates ACH credit entries is the highest expected dollar amount of the entries it delivers to the ACH processor. Credit authorities should be particularly aware that multiple files are often sent to the ACH processor over the several day duration of exposure. This could occur, for instance, if a payroll is divided into separate groupings for executive pay and other salaried employees. Multiple files also occur when the corporation uses a daily cycle for EDI payments.

The calculation below describes how a bank can measure its maximum exposure to an individual corporate customer.

Exposure = (maximum dollar amount of day 0 entries)
+
(total dollar amount of any Day 1 and Day 2)
entries sent the ACH processor)

For example, a company that originates daily corporate vendor payments, in amounts no higher than $30,000 per day, also originates a weekly payroll of $85,000 each Wednesday for payday on Friday. If the company declares bankruptcy late Friday, the bank providing the ACH service could lose $175,000.

ACH files originated Tuesday	No loss
(funded Thursday before bankruptcy)	
ACH files originated Wednesday	$30,000
	$85,000
ACH files originated Thursday	$30,000
ACH files originated Friday	$30,000
(If distributed before bankruptcy)	
Exposure	$175,000

Risk Control Options

It is useful to look at risk control for ACH credit origination in the context of the stages of evolution: Should exposures be prevented before they occur, or is it sufficient to monitor exposures after the fact? But first, let's look at the ways in which the ACH credit origination exposure can be reduced or eliminated before Stage II or Stage III controls are even considered.

Prefunding

The most effective risk reduction or elimination technique for ACH credit origination is to require the bank's corporate customer to prefund the amount of its ACH credit entries. Under a prefunding arrangement, the company is required to have sufficient funds on deposit prior to the time the bank releases the ACH credit entries to the ACH processor—at least one day, and possibly several days, before the payment date. Prefunding can completely eliminate the credit risk associated with ACH credit origination, and consequently, it can eliminate much of the need for expensive credit risk controls.

However, there are two significant obstacles to prefunding. The first is competitive pressure. It is very difficult to require customers to prefund if the bank's competitor down the street does not. Prefunding is very unattractive to a customer because funds that would normally be put to productive use are now forced to lie idle for a day or more. One way to mitigate the problem is for the bank to place the funds in an interest bearing account, or to allow the newly idle funds to be used as compensation for services. Nevertheless, this is a tough sell against a competitor that does not require prefunding.

System considerations in some banks can also make prefunding as difficult and expensive to operate as interactive controls. Balance verification just prior to distribution of credit entries to the ACH processor does not guarantee that the funds will still be in the customer's disbursement account on the payment date several days later. The equivalent of a hold must be placed on the funds over the duration of the exposure. This is often difficult for many banks to accomplish without exception processing. Depending on the bank, a separate dedicated account could be necessary, especially if interest is to be paid. It is also important to be sure that the method selected provides clear access to the funds by the bank in the event of the customer's bankruptcy. If the funds can be frozen by a bankruptcy court, the whole prefunding exercise is for naught.

Because of these obstacles, if prefunding is used at all, it is usually applied only to a selected subset of riskier customers who have been assigned the poorest credit ratings. Some banks are considering requiring prefunding for new ungraded customers for an initial start-up period, perhaps six months or a year. The motivation here is more to prevent fraud than credit losses. Some banks have suffered ACH losses where the perpetrator forms a small shell company and opens an operating account through an unsuspecting branch office. The account is then used once to originate a file of fraudulent credit entries before the perpetrator disappears.

Collateral or Guarantees

A variation on the theme of prefunding is to require collateral or guarantees. This is usually easier to implement from an operations viewpoint, but it does not always provide the complete protection that prefunding does. There is always a possibility that the size of the file of credit entries originated could exceed the amount collateralized or guaranteed. Nevertheless, collateral or guarantees provide a large measure of protection and should be considered a serious alternative to prefunding.

Competitive pressure is again the most difficult obstacle. Requiring collateral, or even partial collateral, may make sense from a risk perspective, but the option is severely limited if competitors are willing to provide the service without collateral or guarantees. In some cases the only viable option is to not offer the service to customers deemed too risky.

Stage II – Periodic Review

Because of the obstacles to prefunding and other forms of collateral and guarantees, banks need other ways to control the risks associated with ACH credit origination. The techniques vary depending upon the bank's stage of risk control evolution and its appetite for expenditures to prevent credit losses.

The backbone of an effective periodic review process is regular management reporting. Monthly reports indicating the dollar exposure of each customer categorized by credit grade serve as a communication vehicle to "know your customer."

In addition to bridging the communication gap usually found between credit administration and operations, regular reporting is necessary to properly support a management policy that requires the periodic review of each customer's total credit exposure. The reporting process should combine information about each customer's creditworthiness with current ACH product usage. Figure 4-3 shows an effective format for those reports. The monthly report lists each customer by credit grade, including a category for ungraded customers, and indicates the total dollars originated and the largest dollar file originated in the last several months. This enables the account officer to examine each customer's recent past exposure, with most attention devoted to low graded and ungraded customers. This usually provides enough time to go back to the customer and negotiate steps to reduce the exposure. The actions could include requiring the customer to prefund its disbursements or to provide collateral or guarantees. It may also mean that the customer should be removed from the service.

Periodic review, with the appropriate follow-up plans and procedures in place, is sufficient control for the vast majority of banks who offer ACH credit origination services.

Stage III – Interactive Control

Unlike periodic review, which brings exposures to management attention after their occurrence, interactive control prevents unauthorized exposures before they occur. ACH credit origination readily lends itself to interactive control, but not without cost.

**Figure 4-3   Monthly Risk Management Report—
ACH Credit Origination**

		Month X		Month X-1	
Account Number	Customer Name	$$ Originated	Largest File	$$ Originated	Largest File
Credit Grade 9					
. . .					
Credit Grade 8					
. . . .					
Credit Grade 1					
. . . .					
Ungraded					
. . . .					

Customer Exposure Limits

The prerequisite to interactive control is the creation of ACH exposure limits for each customer. Credit administration should formalize exposure limits in close consultation with cash management and operations.

Limits should be based on the customer's credit grade or operating need, whichever is more restrictive. Good credit risks should not be given limits higher than their operating needs for specific applications. One reason is that the chances of catching fraudulent entries are higher with tight limits. Special attention is needed when the customer relationship includes multiple subsidiaries or divisions.

How often should limits be reviewed? ACH exposure limits should be part of the normal credit review process, but there are several events that should trigger earlier reviews. One is a change in credit grade. A downgrading should trigger an immediate review of that customer's ACH limit, and depending on the severity of the problem, the contingency action steps mentioned above may have to be invoked as well. Again, the key is timely communication between credit administration, operations, and cash management.

Limits should also be reviewed when overlimit situations are frequently encountered. Increased ACH activity by a high graded customer may warrant a higher limit. Not only are operational difficulties created when limits are too tight, but customer service could be adversely affected as well.

Overlimit Blocks

ACH exposure limits can be active or passive. Active limits, as a matter of policy, block processing of overlimit files until they are released with credit officer approval. Passive limits create a notification of overlimit situations, but do not actually block execution. As a practical matter, passive limits are often installed as a first step toward implementing active overlimit blocks.

Software development cost in operations and the cost of a credit referral system are the main implementation issues for active overlimit blocks. Each bank has to make its own business decision by weighing current and expected exposures against the cost of control.

One way to ease the transition to overlimit blocks is to start with operating limits that are designed to reduce the risk of fraud. This can be done completely within the jurisdiction of the operations department, without the necessity of asking account officers to establish credit limits. To reduce fraud risk, each customer should be assigned a limit by ACH operations, above which no file will be distributed. The limits should be determined by operations or cash management based upon the history of recent file sizes. If a file limit is exceeded, the customer should be called by operations to verify the validity of the file. Besides limiting fraud risk, this practice can help control for credit risk if large increases in file sizes are brought to the account officer's attention.

Once operating limits are in place, credit limits and a referral system for account officers to approve exceptions could then be established. One way to ease the transition is to require credit limits and referrals for approval for watch list customers only. Each watch list customer should be assigned a credit limit per file, as well as a cumulative daily limit, above which no file will be distributed to the ACH network. The watch list approach could then be expanded to include all customers if management determined that interactive control was necessary for all customers.

Figure 4-4 expands the suggested management reporting to reflect customer exposure limits and credit referrals that occur with interactive control.

Risk Assessment Worksheet

The Risk Assessment Worksheet in Figure 4-5 can help a bank assess the aggregate ACH credit origination risk it incurs across the customer base and help determine the level of risk control it needs.

Section I summarizes the magnitude and duration of the total potential exposure for the ACH credit origination product line over the past month. The potential exposure is categorized as either overnight exposure or exposure lasting two or more days. The dollar magnitude of the files the bank delivered to the ACH network can usually be obtained with little difficulty from reports normally produced by the ACH operations area.

Section II summarizes the risk reduction techniques and risk controls that are currently being used, including prefunding, collateral, guarantees, and any Stage III interactive control procedures that block overlimit transactions before they occur.

Section III calculates the bank's net aggregate exposure after considering the impact of risk reduction and risk controls already in place.

Section IV analyzes the creditworthiness of the remaining customer base to provide an indication of the likelihood that the bank will suffer a

Figure 4-4   **Monthly Risk Management Report (Expanded)—ACH Credit Origination**

		Month X				Month X-1			
Acct #	Cust Name	$$ Orig	Large File	Limit	# Refers	$$ Orig	Large File	Limit	# Refers

Credit Grade 10

Credit Grade 9

Credit Grade 1

Ungraded

Figure 4-5   Risk Assessment Worksheet—ACH Credit Origination

---

I. POTENTIAL EXPOSURE

	Number of Customers	Dollars Originated/Month
Overnight exposure	_____	_____
2-day+ exposure	_____	_____
Total	_____	_____

II. CURRENT RISK CONTROLS

(Higher Risk)   (Lower Risk)

Prefunding, collateral, or guarantees?

☐ None   ☐ Selected accounts   ☐ Many Accounts

ACH credit limits established?

☐ None   ☐ Selected accounts   ☐ Many Accounts

Processing blocked if over limit?

☐ No   ☐ Yes, active limits until
                                                                    referred for credit approval

Comments:

_____

_____

_____

III. EXPOSURE AFTER CONTROLS

	Number of Customers	Dollars Originated/Month
Potential Exposure (from Section I.)	_____	_____
Less: prefunded customers	_____	_____
Less: customers with collateral	_____	_____
Less: customers with guarantees	_____	_____
Net Exposure		_____

Figure 4-5 (Continued)

IV. LIKELIHOOD OF LOSS

WATCH LIST CREDIT GRADES

List all watch list customers, except those where exposure has been eliminated with prefunding, collateral or guarantees.

Customer Name	Dollars Originated/Month	Maximum $ File Size
_____	_____	_____
_____	_____	_____
_____	_____	_____
_____	_____	_____

Total Originated/Month _____	Percent of Net Exposure ___%

MEDIUM CREDIT GRADES

Total Originated/Month _____	Percent of Net Exposure ___%

List 5 Largest

_____	_____	_____
_____	_____	_____
_____	_____	_____
_____	_____	_____

HIGHEST CREDIT GRADES

Total Originated/Month _____	Percent of Net Exposure ___%

List 3 Largest

_____	_____	_____
_____	_____	_____
_____	_____	_____

UNGRADED CUSTOMERS

Total Originated/Month _____	Percent of Net Exposure ___%

List 5 Largest

_____	_____	_____
_____	_____	_____
_____	_____	_____
_____	_____	_____

Figure 4-5 (Continued)

V. OTHER FACTORS

(Higher Risk)   (Lower Risk)

Transaction Type?

☐ High dollar vendor payments   ☐ Low dollar payments   ☐ Payroll

Volume growth rate?

☐ Rapid growth   ☐ Stable   ☐ Declining

Fraud or operational risks?

☐ High potential   ☐ Low

Comments:

_____

_____

_____

_____

_____

---

loss. The total credit entries for the month and the largest credit file each customer delivers to the bank that month are categorized by credit grade. Each individual watch list customer is listed with its potential exposure, and customers in the better credit grades with high dollar exposure are also individually listed.

Nonborrowing customers are often a substantial portion of the ACH credit origination customer base, and their unknown creditworthiness is an important complicating factor. They present serious assessment problems because some could be as risky as those on the watch list. If the number of ungraded customers is too large to allow the individual listing of each customer on the worksheet, list those who create the most exposure.

The difficulty in matching product customer lists with credit grade data in an automated fashion was noted in Chapter 2. Even if the task requires a manual effort, accurate matching of information maintained by ACH operations and credit administration is essential for an effective analysis.

Section *V* looks at other less tangible factors that should be considered in a complete risk assessment. One example is the impact of the actual application or transaction type. Payroll may be more likely to be funded by a company in a liquidity crisis, for instance, than vendor payments. Another example of a less tangible factor is the growth rate the product has been experiencing. Management might consider rapidly growing EDI payments to be more risky to the bank than a steady core of payments.

Finally, the choice of control procedure should be influenced by more than the level of credit risk. Credit risk alone may not be sufficient to justify the expenditures needed to prevent exposures before they occur, but combined with the risk of processing fraudulent transactions, more expensive Stage II interactive controls might be justified.

Risk Management Plan

When the risk assessment is completed, the results of the analysis should be the raw material for a comprehensive risk management plan.

Figure 4-6 illustrates the general construct of a sample risk management plan for ACH credit origination. Action plans for each bank will vary considerably, depending upon the bank's level of ACH activity, technical capability, and credit administration policies. The plan should include approval procedures, required controls, and action steps for customers with deteriorating credit quality.

A system to immediately communicate changes in the status of customers with deteriorating credit is vital. Notification of downgrades should not wait for the next monthly report. In addition to an early notification procedure, contingency action steps should be established for deteriorating credits. The plan should include alternatives to consider and an escalation list of people and phone numbers needed to execute the actions at any time of day or night.

The assumption in Figure 4-6 is that the bank does not have an automated system for Stage III interactive control. Prefunding is required for all customers graded 6-9—credit risk is thus eliminated and no further control is required. Grade 5 customers require interactive control via manual procedures, and grade 1-4 customers require periodic review only.

Figure 4-6   Risk Management Plan—ACH Credit Origination

Sample Illustration

	Grades 6-9	Grade 5	Grades 1-4
Approval Required	No new customer approvals	Group manager Monthly review	Normal lending authority Annual review
Operation	Account administrator (Check prefunding)	Credit limits, overlimit blocks Account administrator (Check credit limits, call for credit approvals)	Standard
Credit Exposure Reduction	Prefund, or Collateral, or Guarantee	Partial collateral, or Partial guarantee	
Credit Exposure	None	Credit limit (entries released) less partial collateral or guarantee	Entries released to ACH
Operating Risk	Failure to check prefunding	Failure to check limits	

Action Steps for Deteriorating Credit:

1. When the account officer is informed of a downgrading, immediately notify the officer-in-charge of cash management.
2. The account officer and officer-in-charge of cash management will determine action jointly with others as needed (e.g. , loan administration, legal, loan workout, operations, etc.). Possible actions include:

   A. In bankruptcy, immediately notify operations to cancel transmission of files to the ACH processor.

   B. Negotiate prefunding. Consider an interest bearing account or application toward required balances. Consult operations because exception processing may be required.

   C. Negotiate collateral, partial collateral, or guarantee.

   D. Discontinue service.
3. Cash management will immediately notify operations of actions required.

Receiving ACH Credits

Examples of ACH credit entries a bank could receive include those for its:

- Retail customers who are enrolled in direct deposit of payroll or social security; and
- Corporate customers who receive trade payments from other corporations, including EDI payments with addenda records containing remittance detail.

There is some credit risk in receiving ACH credits since ACH credit entries are provisional and can be recalled by the Federal Reserve if the originating bank fails. In that event, there is a risk that the bank's customer could have withdrawn the funds and might be unable or unwilling to reimburse the bank for the recalled credit.

According to Article 4A of the Uniform Commercial Code, the receiving bank must give prior notice to its customers that the ACH credit entries they receive are provisional. Without prior notification, the bank is not legally entitled to a refund from its customer.

ACH Debit Origination

Banks also offer their corporate customers a wide variety of ACH debit origination services for both consumer and corporate applications.

Typical small dollar services that target the corporate customer's consumer base include direct debiting of individual accounts for insurance premiums, mortgage and loan payments, charitable contributions, and health club payments.

Cash concentration is a very widely used ACH service and the best example of a large dollar ACH debit application. Some companies are also exploring the use of ACH debits for corporate EDI payments.

Consumer Example - Direct Debit

Direct debit services enable companies to collect low dollar, high volume payments directly from consumer accounts at financial institutions throughout the country. The service provides for the electronic transfer of funds from each individual's account to the company's corporate demand deposit account using ACH debits.

The company must obtain authorization from its individual customers to debit their accounts electronically according to an agreed upon payment schedule. According to NACHA rules, the bank that originates ACH debits warrants to the receiving banks that the transactions have been authorized.

Several days prior to the payment date, the company transmits an electronic file of payment orders or delivers a magnetic tape to its bank containing the amount to be debited from each customer account, along with the appropriate payment dates, routing numbers, and account numbers. After extracting "on-us" items, the bank delivers the payment file to the Federal Reserve or private ACH processor. The debit transactions move through the ACH network and are applied by each receiving financial institution to the consumer accounts on the payment date. The originating bank credits the company's collection account on the payment date, and most banks grant the company funds availability in the morning of the payment date.

Corporate Example - Cash Concentration

Cash concentration services enable companies to concentrate funds from multiple accounts at other financial institutions into one concentration account at the originating bank. Funds can be concentrated from geographically dispersed retail stores, branches, subsidiaries, lock boxes, or other field locations to which the company's customers send remittances. The concentrated funds, which might otherwise lie idle, can be used for timely funding of disbursements and investments or to pay down debt.

At the end of each business day, each location reports the day's deposit information to a data collection facility. Some companies do their own data collection via telephone or their own electronic link to each location, but often the data collection is performed by a third-party vendor under contract to either the bank or the company. In other cases, the bank will provide the data collection facility using its own technology. When the bank receives the transmission of deposit information by a predetermined cut-off time, it creates a file of ACH debits and delivers it to the Federal Reserve or private ACH processor that evening. The debit transactions move through the ACH network and are posted by each local bank the next business day. The originating bank credits the company's concentration account and provides morning funds availability.

Credit Risk Description

Consumer Direct Debit

There is return item risk for each consumer account debited, not unlike the return item risk associated with checks. An ACH debit can be returned by the local receiving bank for a variety of reasons, including insufficient funds, wrong account number, account closed, and others. The Federal Reserve can also return the items if the local bank fails. Unlike check returns, Regulation E also gives the consumer 60 days to notify the bank of an unauthorized ACH debit transfer or a transfer made in error.

Normally, returned debits are not a problem because the bank will charge them back to the company's account. In the event of a bankruptcy, however, the company's account may be frozen or may not have sufficient funds to cover the chargeback, and the originating bank could suffer a loss. Nevertheless, return exposure to a diverse group of consumer accounts with small-dollar transactions is usually minimal, and the return rate can usually be predicted with confidence based on past history. The exposure is somewhat limited because the receiving bank only has until midnight of the business day following receipt of the debit to decide to return the item.

However, the consumer's right of recision for up to 60 days adds considerable risk. This is particularly true if the consumer has paid the company in advance and the company is providing poor service or has otherwise alienated its consumers. In this case, there is a significant danger that a large number of consumers would exercise their right of recision and ask their bank to return items going back 60 days.

Cash Concentration

Unlike consumer direct debit, where there is a diversity of unrelated individual accounts being debited, the company owns all of the accounts at the local banks from which funds are concentrated. Therefore, the return item risk is that *all* debit items would be returned if the company declares bankruptcy. If the company withdraws the concentrated funds when they are made available at the opening of business, and the company declares bankruptcy later in the day, the local accounts would be frozen and all of the ACH debits would be returned.

Customer Risk Calculation

The general sequence of events outlined in Figure 4-7 creates the return item exposure associated with all ACH debit origination, but the calculation of a bank's maximum exposure to its corporate customer depends upon the specific debit application.

Consumer Direct Debit – Daily Files

Many direct debit applications involve the origination of debit files on a daily basis. In those cases, the calculation of the return item exposure is similar to daily check deposits.

$$\text{Exposure} = (\text{ maximum \$ amount of daily file }) \times$$
$$(\text{ maximum number days to return }) \times (\text{ return rate })$$

For example, assume that a company has a large consumer customer base with a billing cycle that distributes debit files evenly over the month in

---

Figure 4-7   ACH Debit Origination

DAY 0	DAY 1	DAY 2	DAY 2 or 3	DAY 4 or 5
Company sends ACH debit file to bank.	Bank makes funds available to company.		Regional banks return ACH debits - account frozen.	Bank receives returned ACH debits.
Bank extracts "on us" and delivers file to Federal Reserve.	ACH debits received by local banks.	Company declares bankruptcy.		Bank has unsecured claim against company.
	Bank Fed account is credited.			Bank Fed account is debited.
		Bank Exposure		

Source: NACHA

amounts of no more than $25,000 per day. The bank experiences a historical return rate of about 2.5% due to insufficient funds. If the company is unable to meet its financial obligations and does not provide funding for the bank's chargeback for returned debits, the bank could lose $2,500.

($25,000) × (4 days to return) × (0.25 return rate) = $2,500

Unlike daily check deposits, there is a much more serious risk for the originating bank. If the same company provides poor service, and an estimated 30% of its consumers exercise their right of recision, the bank could lose $450,000!

($25,000) × (60 days to return) × (0.3 return rate) = $450,000

Consumer Direct Debit – Weekly Files

The return times for ACH debit entries vary with the actual customer base, and to some extent with the ACH processor, but four days is a reasonable average return time to assume. If the company originates debit files less frequently than every four days, return time is not a factor in calculating credit exposure.

Exposure = (maximum $ amount of daily file) × (return rate)

For example, if the company originated a weekly file of $125,000 instead of daily files, the bank could lose $3,125 if the company declared bankruptcy immediately after the file enters the ACH network.

($125,000) × (0.025 return rate) = $3,125

The bank might lose nothing, however, if the company were to declare bankruptcy five days later—after funding all of the bank's chargebacks.

If the company's consumers exercise their right of recision, extending the return time to 60 days, which is well beyond the weekly origination cycle, the bank would still lose close to $450,000.

Cash Concentration

Since all of the debits are expected to be returned in the event of a bankruptcy with cash concentration, the historical return rate is not a factor in calculating credit exposure to a customer. Besides the amount concentrated, the key variable is the number of days it takes to return an ACH debit. Since NACHA rules require that debits over $2,500 must be returned by the receiving bank no later than the night cycle deadline of the next banking day, some banks assume that it will take three days to receive cash concentration returns.

$$\text{Exposure} = (\text{maximum } \$ \text{ amount of daily file}) \times (\text{maximum number days to return})$$

For example, a retailer with 14 store locations concentrates $25,000 per day from each local store. Total funds concentrated is, therefore, $350,000 per day. In a bankruptcy, all of the concentration debits would likely be returned, so the bank could lose $1,050,000.

$$(\$300,000) \times (3 \text{ days to return}) = \$1,050,000$$

Risk Control Options

We saw that with prefunding and Stage III controls, banks can limit credit origination exposure before it occurs. However, the options are more limited with debit origination because the exposure is caused by an uncertain stream of future return items that occur well after the commitment of credit. Stage III controls are largely impractical. Nevertheless, there are important steps that can be taken to control the risk.

As with credit origination, the base level of exposure can be reduced with diligent credit analysis and approval procedures before investment in Stage II and Stage III controls are even considered. Because of the potential for very large exposures for cash concentration and some consumer direct debit applications, the first line of defense should be very stringent credit approval hurdles.

Collateral or Guarantees

Some customers with less than acceptable creditworthiness may be eligible to use the service after negotiating arrangements for collateral or guarantees. Most commonly, collateral or guarantees are required for existing customers with deteriorating credit. New customers are more likely to be rejected completely for credit reasons, and even if the customer was acceptable to the bank with collateral or partial collateral, the competition would likely make the prospect extremely remote.

Stage II – Periodic Review

Because the automated techniques for preventing exposures before they occur are limited, very diligent periodic review is the most important risk control measure available for ACH debit origination. The backbone of an effective periodic review process is regular monthly reporting that indicates the dollar exposure of each customer categorized by credit grade.

Consumer Direct Debit

The important variables for consumer direct debit are the return rate and the dollar value of returns by customer. Figure 4-8 shows an effective format for monthly reports to present that information. The account officer should review the reports carefully for significant changes and go back to the customer for explanations. Why are returns increasing? Is the company's consumer base deteriorating? Why? Is the company's level of service declining? Why? Most importantly, is there any danger that the return rate could explode with large numbers of consumers exercising 60 day right of recision?

It is critical that the monthly report serves as a vehicle to allow, or force, the account officer to initiate preventative action before returns become unacceptable. Companies with deteriorating credit quality require even closer attention and should be tracked more frequently than monthly.

Short of removing the customer from the service or requiring collateral, the account officer should consider delaying availability if the return rate or credit quality is deteriorating. Companies with deteriorating credit may want to avoid disrupting their customers' payment routine and continue the service by negotiating a delayed availability schedule. Most of the bank's return item exposure can be eliminated by delaying availability four or more days instead of allowing the company to withdraw the funds on the payment date. The actual level of protection depends upon the bank's return experience with that company, and it should be carefully considered before negotiating an availability schedule. Remember, also, that delayed availability will not offer protection from a large number of consumers who exercise their 60 day right of recision.

Figure 4-8   **Monthly Risk Management Report—**
ACH Consumer Direct Debit

		Month X				Month X-1				(Optional) Average # Days to Return
Acct #	Cust Name	$$ Orig	Max File	Ret. Rate	$$ Ret	$$ Orig	Max File	Ret. Rate	$$ Ret	to Return
Credit Grade 9										
· · ·										
Credit Grade 8										
° · · ·										
Credit Grade 1										
· · · · · · · ·										
Ungraded										
· · ·										

The sample report in Figure 4-8 has an optional column to indicate average and maximum number of days to return for each customer, but the practical reality is that most banks would find this difficult to report on a regular basis. Since the most important use for this information is in the rare instances when delayed availability is being negotiated, it might better be obtained on an exception basis only.

Cash Concentration

The periodic review techniques for cash concentration are different than consumer direct debit because the entire debit file is at risk. Figure 4-9 shows a sample report that indicates the dollar amounts of the average and peak cash concentration files originated over the past month.

As with direct debit, it is critical that the monthly report is used by the account officer to initiate preventative action before the credit risk becomes unacceptable. Companies with deteriorating credit quality require more frequent review than monthly.

The action steps that should be considered for weak credit risks include negotiation for collateral, guarantees, or delayed availability, as above. In addition, an option for cash concentration that is not available for consumer direct debit is to replace the ACH debits with wire transfers. Unlike ACH debits, wire transfers are final when executed, so the return item risk is completely eliminated.

If complete conversion to wire transfer is not feasible because of a prohibitively large number of locations, consider placing only the highest average dollar locations on wire transfer and continue to allow ACH for the remaining locations. A variation on that theme is to negotiate ACH limits for each location and require the company to wire funds over the limit.

Stage III – Interactive Control

Setting limits above which wire transfers are required is a form of interactive control that will prevent unapproved exposures before they occur.

If the bank uses a third-party data collection vendor, limits can usually be implemented by the vendor. If a company location reports a deposit that exceeds a limit, the vendor will reject the concentration request. The company would then be responsible for initiating a wire transfer from the rejected local account to the concentration account. If the company does its own data collection, or if the company has contracted a third-party vendor,

**Figure 4-9   Monthly Risk Management Report—
                  ACH Cash Concentration**

		Month X		Month X-1	
Account Number	Customer Name	$$ Originated	Largest File	$$ Originated	Largest File
Credit Grade 9					
·					
·					
·					
Credit Grade 8					
·					
·					
·					
·					
Credit Grade 1					
·					
·					
·					
·					
·					
·					
·					
·					
Ungraded					
·					
·					
·					
·					

the bank will have to have the systems in place to block transactions that exceed the limit and notify the company that a wire transfer is required.

The interactive controls that are available for consumer direct debit applications are similar to those discussed for ACH credit origination. In brief summary, credit administration can establish customer exposure limits in close consultation with cash management and operations. The limits should reflect the customer's creditworthiness and should not exceed the customer's operating need. Overlimit blocks can be established to prevent processing ACH files that exceed the established limits. Credit approval would be required before the file is processed.

Risk Assessment Worksheet

Risk Assessment Worksheets are found in Figures 4-10 and 4-11 for consumer direct debit and cash concentration respectively. They are designed to help a bank assess the aggregate ACH debit origination risk it incurs across each customer base, and they provide checklists to help the bank focus on the most important risk factors.

Section I in Figures 4-10 and 4-11 summarizes the magnitude and duration of the total potential exposure for the consumer direct debit and cash concentration product lines over the past month. The dollar magnitude of the debit files the bank delivered to the ACH network can usually be obtained with little difficulty from reports normally produced by the ACH operations area. Return statistics are also needed for measuring consumer direct debit risk.

Section II summarizes the risk reduction techniques and risk controls that are currently being used, including collateral, guarantees, and Stage II periodic review procedures.

Section III calculates the bank's net aggregate exposure after considering the impact of risk reduction and risk controls already in place.

Section IV analyzes the creditworthiness of the remaining customer base to provide an indication of the likelihood that the bank will suffer a loss. For consumer direct debit, the total dollars returned for the month are categorized by credit grade. For cash concentration, the total dollars originated are categorized by credit grade along with the largest debit file each customer delivers to the bank (times three days to receive return items). Individual watch list customers are listed with their potential exposure, and

**Figure 4-10   Risk Assessment Worksheet—
ACH Consumer Direct Debit**

I. POTENTIAL EXPOSURE

Number of Customers: _____
Dollars Originated/Month: _____

Note: Total is at risk only in
the extremely unlikely event
that 100 percent of
consumers exercise their
right of recision.

Dollars Returned/Month: _____

II. CURRENT RISK CONTROLS

(Higher Risk)   (Lower Risk)

Collateral or guarantees?

☐ None   ☐ Selected accounts

Formal risk monitoring?

☐ No formal process   ☐ Regular monthly
                                     reporting

Comments:

_____
_____
_____
_____
_____

III. EXPOSURE AFTER CONTROLS

	No. Customers	$ Originated/Mo.	$ Returned/Mo.
Potential Exposure (from Section I.)	_____	_____	_____
Less: customers with collateral	_____	_____	_____
Less: customers with guarantees	_____	_____	_____

Net (Return) Exposure	_____

Figure 4-10 (Continued)

IV. <u>LIKELIHOOD OF LOSS</u>

WATCH LIST CREDIT GRADES

List all watch list customers, except those where exposure has been eliminated with collateral or guarantees.

<u>Customer Name</u>	<u>Dollars Originated/Month</u>	<u>DollarsReturned/Month</u>
_____	_____	_____
_____	_____	_____
_____	_____	_____
_____	_____	_____

Total Returned/Month	_____	Percent of Net Exposure ____%

MEDIUM CREDIT GRADES

Total Returned/Month	_____	Percent of Net Exposure ____%

List 5 Largest

_____	_____	_____
_____	_____	_____
_____	_____	_____
_____	_____	_____

HIGHEST CREDIT GRADES

Total Returned/Month	_____	Percent of Net Exposure ____%

List 3 Largest

_____	_____	_____
_____	_____	_____

UNGRADED CUSTOMERS

Total Returned/Month	_____	Percent of Net Exposure ____%

List 5 Largest

_____	_____	_____
_____	_____	_____
_____	_____	_____
_____	_____	_____

Figure 4-10 (Continued)

V. OTHER FACTORS

(Higher Risk)   (Lower Risk)

Customer Experience?

❏ New start-up   ❏ Stable, long term
                                                       customer

Importance to Consumer (TransactionType)?

❏ Health club membership   ❏ Mixed   ❏ Mortgage payments
    Charitable contributions   Insurance premiums

Volume growth rate?

❏ Rapid growth   ❏ Stable

Fraud or operational risks?

❏ High potential   ❏ Low

Comments:

_____

_____

_____

_____

Figure 4-11   Risk Assessment Worksheet—ACH Cash Concentration

I. POTENTIAL EXPOSURE

Number of Customers: _____

Dollars Originated/Month: _____

II. CURRENT RISK CONTROLS

(Higher Risk)   (Lower Risk)

Collateral or guarantees?

☐ None   ☐ Selected accounts

Formal risk monitoring?

☐ No formal process   ☐ Regular monthly
                                             reporting

Comments:

_____
_____
_____
_____
_____

III. EXPOSURE AFTER CONTROLS

	Number of Customers	Dollars Originated/Month
Potential Exposure (from Section I.)	_____	_____
Less: customers with collateral	_____	_____
Less: customers with guarantees	_____	_____
Net Exposure		_____

Figure 4-11 (Continued)

IV. LIKELIHOOD OF LOSS

WATCH LIST CREDIT GRADES

List all watch list customers, except those where exposure has been eliminated with collateral or guarantees.

Customer Name	Dollars Originated/Mo.	Max. $ File Size	Times 4 Days to Return
_____	_____	_____	_____
_____	_____	_____	_____
_____	_____	_____	_____
_____	_____	_____	_____

Total Originated/Month	_____	Percent of Net Exposure	____%

MEDIUM CREDIT GRADES

Total Originated/Month	_____	Percent of Net Exposure	____%

List 5 Largest

_____	_____	_____	_____
_____	_____	_____	_____
_____	_____	_____	_____
_____	_____	_____	_____

HIGHEST CREDIT GRADES

Total Originated/Month	_____	Percent of Net Exposure	____%

List 3 Largest

_____	_____	_____	_____
_____	_____	_____	_____
_____	_____	_____	_____

UNGRADED CUSTOMERS

Total Originated/Month	_____	Percent of Net Exposure	____%

List 5 Largest

_____	_____	_____	_____
_____	_____	_____	_____
_____	_____	_____	_____
_____	_____	_____	_____

Figure 4-11 (Continued)

V. OTHER FACTORS

(Higher Risk)   (Lower Risk)

Return item experience?

☐ Some NSF returns   ☐ No NSF returns

Volume growth rate?

☐ Rapid growth   ☐ Stable

Fraud or operational risks?

☐ High potential   ☐ Low

Comments:

_____

_____

_____

_____

customers in the better credit grades with high dollar exposure are also individually listed.

The unknown creditworthiness of nonborrowing customers can be an important complicating factor. They present serious assessment problems because some could be as risky as those on the watch list. If the number of ungraded customers is too large to allow the individual listing of each customer on the worksheet, list those who create the most exposure.

Section V looks at other less tangible factors that should be considered in a complete risk assessment. For example, the transaction type and its importance to the consumer is an important factor when assessing consumer direct debit risk. A consumer is more likely to make sure good funds are available for a life insurance premium than a charitable contribution. Likewise, health club payments are more likely to be returned under the 60 day right of recision than mortgage payments. The company's experience with direct debit and the stability of transaction volumes are also important factors.

Finally, analysis of credit risk alone may not lead to the best decision. The potential for fraud and operational losses, although outside the scope of this book, should be thoroughly explored.

Risk Management Plan

Figures 4-12 and 4-13 illustrate the general outline of sample risk management plans for consumer direct debit and cash concentration respectively. Each bank should carefully construct its own plan based upon its own risk assessment and its own trade-offs between potential loss and the cost of various levels of risk control. The important point is that the results are documented and enforced.

Receiving ACH Debits

Examples of ACH credit entries a bank could receive include those for its:

- Retail customers who pay insurance premium, mortgage, or health club payments automatically; and
- Corporate customers who receive cash concentration debits because they are concentrating funds to an account at another financial institution.

There is no unavoidable credit risk to the receiving bank because debits can be returned for insufficient funds. Nevertheless, the bank has to make a credit decision as to whether to initiate a return due to insufficient funds.

If the bank decides to accept the credit risk and pay over insufficient funds, there is an additional operational risk to face. For example, if the bank accepts a debit that creates an overdraft, it is possible that the receiving company could subsequently notify the bank that the debit was unauthorized. If the bank was notified after the return deadline, an attempt to return the debit would likely be dishonored as a late return.

Wire Transfer

Wire transfers are used for very high dollar payments where security and finality of payment are of paramount importance. The two main wire

Figure 4-12   Risk Management Plan—ACH Consumer Direct Debit

Sample Illustration

	Grades 6-9	Grade 5	Grades 1-4
Approval Required	No new customer approvals	Group manager Monthly review	Normal lending authority Annual review
Operation	Credit limits, overlimit blocks Account administrator (Check credit limits)	Credit limits, overlimit blocks Account administrator (Check credit limits)	Standard
Credit Exposure Reduction	Delay availability 4+ days, or Require collateral for returns, or Require guarantee	Delay availability 1-3 days, or Require partial collateral, or Partial Guarantee	
Credit Exposure	None	Portion of returns	All returns
Operating Risk	Failure to check limits		

Action Steps for Deteriorating Credit:

1. When the account officer is informed of a downgrading, immediately notify the officer-in-charge of cash management.
2. The account officer and officer-in-charge of cash management will determine action jointly with others as needed (e.g., loan administration, legal, loan workout, operations, etc.). Possible actions include:
    A. Delay availability.
    B. Negotiate collateral, partial collateral, or guarantee.
    C. Discontinue service.
3. Cash management will immediately notify operations of actions required.

Figure 4-13   Risk Management Plan—ACH Cash Concentration

Sample Illustration

	Grades 6-9	Grade 5	Grades 1-4
Approval Required	No new customer approvals	Group manager Monthly review	Normal lending authority Annual review
Operation	Account administrator (Check location and file limits) Location limits, file limits	Account administrator (Check location and file limits) Location limits, file limits	Standard
Credit Exposure Reduction	Delay availability 3 days, or Require wire transfer, or Require 3 day's collateral, or Require guarantee	Partial collateral, or Partial guarantee	
Credit Exposure	None	Portion of returns	All returns
Operating Risk	Failure to check limits	Failure to check limits	

Action Steps for Deteriorating Credit:

1. When the account officer is informed of a downgrading, immediately notify the officer-in-charge of cash management.
2. The account officer and officer-in-charge of cash management will determine action jointly with others as needed (e.g., loan administration, legal, loan workout, operations, etc.). Possible actions include:
   A. Replace all ACH debits with wire transfer.
   B. Negotiate lower location limits. Wire funds over limit.
   C. Delay availability.
   D. Negotiate collateral, partial collateral, or guarantee.
   E. Discontinue service.
3. Cash management will immediately notify operations of actions required.

transfer networks in the United States are Fedwire, operated by the Federal Reserve System, and the Clearing House Interbank Payments System (CHIPS), operated by the New York Clearing House Association. Fedwire and CHIPS account for over 80% of the value of all payments in the United States, even though they account for only a small fraction of 1% of all payment transactions.

Fedwire payments are final when executed because the Federal Reserve assumes the credit risk if there are insufficient funds in the sending bank's Federal Reserve account. Unlike the ACH, payments cannot be recalled if the sending bank fails.

In day-to-day business practice, CHIPS finality is treated by banks and their customers in much the same way as Fedwire, but CHIPS payments are not final until the network participants fund their net obligations at the end of the day. This is done using Fedwire transfers at the close of business. The New York Clearing House Association assures final settlement by requiring that the network participants collateralize the exposure and by limiting exposures with net debit caps and bilateral credit limits.

Outgoing Wires

Banks offer their corporate customers a variety of ways to initiate wire transfers, ranging from simple telephone instructions with call-back security, to totally automated electronic initiation. Many banks encourage companies to initiate wire transfers electronically from a personal computer with bank provided software or software licensed from a third party. Electronic initiation allows the company to create, modify, and approve transfers in a highly structured and secure way. Most services have multiple levels of security that include password access, dual authorizations, and electronic authentication or encryption. Electronic initiation also allows the customer to store repetitive information to minimize time consuming key entry and reduce the possibility of errors.

Credit Risk Description

Outgoing wire transfer can create an intraday overdraft if funds are wired out of a customer's account earlier in the day than covering funds are received. The cover will often be in the form of an incoming wire that is expected later in the day, or it may be projected from the company's normal business receipts over the course of the day. The credit risk is that good funds may not arrive when expected. If the company has severe financial difficulties or declares bankruptcy, an intraday overdraft could become an overnight overdraft or an actual loss.

Risk Control Options

The Federal Reserve's self-assessment guide that banks use to establish their Federal Reserve daylight overdraft cap is a major consideration when banks look at their options for controlling wire transfer risk. The self-assessment process is described in the August 20, 1992, "Comprehensive Federal Reserve Policy Statement on Payments System Risk" which is an updated compilation of previously adopted risk reduction policies.

The self-assessment guide includes an important section on monitoring customer positions (See Appendix A). The section contains an extensive checklist of factors to consider, but the decision to rate a bank's customer monitoring as strong, satisfactory, or unsatisfactory is left to the bank—subject to approval by the bank's board of directors and review by the examiners. In basic terms, the bank has to decide to what degree interactive controls are necessary.

Stage II – Periodic Review

An established periodic review process will provide the information necessary to determine if, and to what degree, interactive control is necessary. Because of the high dollar nature of wire transfer, it is usually the first area considered for interactive control.

Review of customer exposures may occur on a more frequent cycle than other services—sometimes on a daily basis for high dollar users. It makes sense to monitor on two levels: first, to detect which customers regularly use high dollar wire transfers; and secondly, to determine which of those normally incur intraday overdrafts.

Figure 4-14 shows a sample report that indicates the largest users of wire transfer. The report highlights the total dollars wired by each customer for the period and the amount of the largest transaction. As with similar periodic reports for other services, the customers are categorized by credit grade. Figure 4-15 expands the report to include the largest daylight overdraft each customer incurs.

The ability of a bank to monitor daylight overdrafts depends upon its demand deposit accounting technology. A bank that memo posts transactions to its DDA system as they occur during the day will know which customers create intraday overdrafts—if the system is accurate. Accuracy depends upon the completeness of the range of transaction types the system

**Figure 4-14   Monthly Risk Management Report
Outgoing Wire Transfer**

Account Number	Customer Name	Month X		Month X-1	
		$$ Total Wires	Largest Wire	$$ Total Wires	Largest Wire
Credit Grade 9					
· · ·					
Credit Grade 8					
· · · ·					
Credit Grade 1					
· · · · · · · · ·					
Ungraded					
· · · ·					

Figure 4-15   Monthly Risk Management Report
Outgoing Wire Transfer, Daylight Overdrafts

Acct #	Cust Name	$$ Total Wires	Largest Wire	Largest DOD	DOD Limit	# Credit Refers

Credit Grade 10

.						
.						
.						

Credit Grade 9

.						
.						
.						
.						

Credit Grade 1

.						
.						
.						
.						
.						
.						
.						

Ungraded

.						
.						
.						
.						

captures and the timeliness of the data capture. Most systems only capture selected transaction types automatically, starting with incoming and outgoing wire transfers, and gradually adding transaction types (i.e., letter of credit, securities, ACH, check presentments, etc.) as technology and budgets allow.

Stage III – Interactive Controls

Once relatively accurate intraday balances are maintained, interactive controls to block daylight overdrafts before they occur can be implemented. Most banks with interactive controls require the wire transfer department to check the customer's balance and place a hold on the account before an outgoing wire is completed. These "funds control" systems can range from totally manual procedures to the highly automated. If the account does not have sufficient balances to cover the wire request, the account officer is contacted for approval before the wire is released.

Frequently, intraday credit limits can be established for creditworthy customers. With intraday limits, the account officer is contacted for approval only if the available balance plus the intraday limit is insufficient to cover the wire request. The sample periodic report in Figure 4-15 includes columns for a daylight overdraft limit and the number of times the customer's wire request exceeded the limit and required credit referral. Daylight overdraft limits should be reviewed on a regular basis, and customers that are frequently referred for credit approval require special attention to determine if the limit is still appropriate. Is the customer having financial difficulty, or are the operating requirements of a growing, creditworthy customer changing? A downgrading should trigger an immediate review to determine if the customer's limit should be reduced or eliminated.

With or without credit limits, it is important for the account officer to understand the customer's expected activity before outgoing wires are approved. Few funds control systems capture all transactions online, and the intraday balance may not reflect a large transaction the account officer should expect.

Customer Risk Calculation

Even with a highly automated funds control system, the exposure to a specific customer depends on the accuracy of the intraday balance at the time of the credit referral and approval.

$$\text{Exposure} = (\text{ intraday limit })$$
$$+$$
$$(\text{ overlimit approvals })$$
$$+$$
$$(\text{ significant debit transactions that are}$$
$$\text{not memo posted intraday })$$

The calculation is similar for banks with no preapproved intraday credit limits.

$$\text{Exposure} = (\text{ intraday overdraft approvals })$$
$$+$$
$$(\text{ significant debit transactions that are}$$
$$\text{not memo posted intraday })$$

Risk Assessment Worksheet

Appendix A contains the Federal Reserve's self-assessment checklist for monitoring customer positions. Coupled with the distribution of customers by credit grade in Figures 4-14 or 4-15, the checklist is a logical tool for assessing the overall product line risk of outgoing wire transfers.

Risk Management Plan

Figure 4-16 illustrates the general construct of a sample risk management plan for outgoing wire transfer services. Action plans for each bank will vary considerably, depending upon the bank's level of wire transfer activity, technical capability, and credit administration policies. Each bank should carefully construct its own plan based upon its own risk assessment and its own analysis of trade-offs between potential loss and the cost of various levels of control. The sample plan assumes a bank with modest intraday tracking abilities and reliance on largely manual procedures.

Incoming Wires

The bank has no credit risk associated with receiving incoming Fedwires because payments are final when executed. The Federal Reserve assumes the credit risk that the sending bank might have insufficient funds in its Federal Reserve account.

Figure 4-16   **Risk Management Plan—Outgoing Wire Transfer**

Sample Illustration

	Grades 6-9	Grade 5	Grades 1-4
Approval Required	No new customer approvals	Group manager Monthly review	Normal lending authority Annual review
Operation	Refer all wires for account officer approval.	Check balance before releasing wire. Refer overdrafts for approval before releasing wire.	Check balance and/or daylight overdraft limit before releasing wire. Refer overlimit for approval.
Credit Exposure Reduction	Clear good funds required - no daylight overdrafts allowed.	No pre approved daylight overdraft limits allowed.	Daylight overdraft limits allowed only for selected accounts with clear operational need.
Credit Exposure	None	Amount of daylight overdraft approved.	Amount of daylight overdraft limit.
Operating Risk	Failure to check balance. Inaccurate balance displayed.	Failure to check balance. Inaccurate balance displayed.	Failure to check balance and/or daylight overdraft limit. Inaccurate balance displayed.

Action Steps for Deteriorating Credit:

1. When the account officer is informed of a downgrading, immediately notify the officer-in-charge of cash management.
2. The account officer and officer-in-charge of cash management will determine action jointly with others as needed (e.g. , loan administration, legal, loan workout, operations, etc.). Possible actions include:
   A. Reduce or eliminate intraday credit limit, if one exists.
   B. Limit the customer to one account that can be used for outgoing wire transfer and funding transactions only.
   C. Discontinue service.
3. Cash management will immediately notify operations of actions required.

There is an extremely remote possibility that CHIPS could fail to settle despite the stringent controls and collateral requirements placed on CHIPS members. The risk is so remote that it is not a serious factor to consider when accepting CHIPS payments into customer accounts.

Third-Party Access

The Federal Reserve is concerned about the risk to banks who allow third parties like service bureaus, outsourcing processors and corporate originators to send ACH and Fedwire payments directly to the Federal Reserve. The bank incurs the same risks when initiating payments whether or not it physically initiates and processes the transactions. More importantly, the bank's exposure can be greatly magnified unless it receives all the information from the third party that it normally would have if it processed its own work.

The exposures described earlier in this chapter become even more threatening if the bank does not preserve its ability to use all of the periodic review and interactive control techniques that prudent business practice demands. Banks can easily lose sight of the risks they actually incur if they do not focus on the day-to-day process of originating payments.

The Federal Reserve Board currently has a risk reduction policy in place for Fedwire transfers with third-party access (Appendix D). The recent rapid increases in ACH transaction and dollar volume coupled with the growing trend to use third-party processors has caused the Federal Reserve to consider expanding their policies to include ACH credit origination. It is likely that the ACH policy will be modeled after the existing Fedwire policy. Specifically, the Federal Reserve is likely to require banks to take the following actions with respect to credit risk and fraud and operating risk.

Credit Risk

Banks incur credit risk from the time ACH credit entries are released to the ACH—the Federal Reserve in this case—until they are funded by the customer, usually at least a day later. If a third party releases the entries, it is likely that the new Federal Reserve policy will require banks and processors to establish guidelines that ensure that the bank has authorized all of the ACH credit entries before the processor releases the entries. One way for the bank to ensure that proper credit authorization has occurred is to establish credit origination limits for the processor. The bank would preapprove transactions up to a limit, require notification of transactions exceeding the limit, and block release until the bank gives specific approval for transactions exceeding the limit.

The policy will probably require that the bank's Board of Directors must agree to the arrangement, including the specifics of the operational activity and any dollar caps and limitations. They will also probably require a written agreement with the Federal Reserve.

With the prevalence of bank processing affiliates, it is also likely that the Federal Reserve will require that the credit authorization is separated so no one person can control it at both the bank and the processing organization.

Fraud and Operating Risk

Also, expect the policy to require contingency plans in the case of operating error by the third-party processor, inspections by the bank's primary regulator, and regularly scheduled internal audits. See Appendix D for the complete text of the current Fedwire policy.

5

CHECK SERVICES

Despite the rapid growth of electronic funds transfer, check services provide the core revenue and profitability for most bank cash management departments. The U.S. check processing system is highly efficient, and it is becoming more efficient each year. Checks are an ingrown part of our culture that many people are reluctant to part with. Despite the growing efficiency of the system, float and related profit opportunities continue to be strong incentives for both banks and corporations to keep using checks. Overall check usage continues to grow at modest rates.

Check services comprise two major categories of corporate service: check disbursement and check collection. Check disbursement services include all of the standard business checking accounts that banks offer, as well as specialized variations like controlled disbursement and payable through drafts. Check collection encompasses the variety of business deposit services, ranging from highly automated lock boxes to traditional over-the-counter deposits. Some banks offer check collection and disbursement services to correspondent banks in the form of outgoing and incoming cash letters.

Check Disbursement

Unlike initiating irrevocable electronic funds transfers (ACH credit and wire transfer), credit risk does not arise automatically from the mechanics and timing of the check clearance system. A bank always has the option to return checks if there are insufficient funds in the issuing customer's account. Federal Reserve Regulation J permits the return of checks on the business day following presentment.

Nevertheless, a bank can still create credit risk if it decides not to return checks for insufficient funds, on the expectation that its customer will ultimately provide funding. Most banks give very serious consideration before deciding to return a large number of checks because the action could significantly worsen the company's financial situation, or force the company into bankruptcy, and possibly leave the bank vulnerable to creditor suits. It is not unusual for a bank to decide not to return a corporate customer's checks.

Credit Risk Description

The primary risk associated with check disbursement is the possibility that the company could fail to fund the checks presented for payment, either because of bankruptcy or severe liquidity problems. In cases where checks are not returned, the entire check presentment is at risk.

Even if checks are returned, the bank always incurs a small loss of its use of funds. The Federal Reserve always debits the bank's Federal Reserve account on the day the checks are presented for payment. If the bank decides to return the checks the following day, the Federal Reserve will recredit the bank's account the day after it receives the returns—two days after the original presentment debit. The bank loses the use of those funds for two days. This is illustrated in Figure 5-1.

Customer Risk Calculation

The maximum exposure due to this loss of the use of funds is calculated as follows:

Exposure = (maximum Day 0 presentment) × (2 days) × (cost of funds)

+

(maximum Day 1 presentment) × (cost of funds)

Figure 5-1   Controlled Disbursement Return Items

DAY 0	DAY 1	DAY 2
Company's checks clear.	Bank determines company did not fund Day 0 clearings.	Bank Fed account is credited as of Day 2 for returns. They are not backvalued to Day 0 and Day 1.
Bank's Fed account is debited.	Bank returns Day 0 and Day 1 checks.	

For example, assume a company's disbursement checks are presented for payment every day, with a history of daily presentment amounts that are no greater than $35,000. If the company fails to fund its disbursements, and the bank decides to return the checks, the bank will incur a very small loss. If the bank's cost of funds is 10%, the loss will be less than $30.00.

$$(\$35{,}000) \times (2 \text{ days}) \times (0.1 \times \tfrac{1}{360}) = \$19.44$$
$$(\$35{,}000) \times (0.1 \times \tfrac{1}{360}) = \quad 9.72$$

$$\overline{\quad\$29.16\quad}$$

However, if the bank decided to extend credit and pay the checks, the bank could lose the entire $35,000 if the company subsequently declared bankruptcy.

Besides this basic credit risk inherent in all check disbursement, there are other risks associated with controlled disbursement.

Controlled Disbursement

Controlled disbursement continues to grow at healthy rates in many market segments, especially as the treasurers and cash managers of many small and middle market companies strive to improve their cash flows.

Controlled disbursement allows a company to draw checks on a zero balance account and minimize idle balances. The company is notified in the morning, usually no later than 10:00 a.m., of the exact amount needed to fund all checks that will be presented to the bank for payment that day. The service enables the company to determine its cash position and make investment or borrowing decisions in the morning when interest rates are generally more stable.

The main requirement from the bank service provider's perspective is that the bank must be able to use a transit routing number that receives morning check presentments from the Federal Reserve and does not receive presentments from any other source. Over-the-counter deposits, or presentments from correspondent banks later in the day, would make accurate controlled disbursement extremely difficult to offer. Most banks use a separate subsidiary or an affiliate with a separate transit routing number as the controlled disbursement payor bank. To speed the process, the affiliate often receives electronic presentment information from the Federal Reserve before the physical checks are delivered.

Most banks offer the company one of several methods of funding:

- Automated book transfer from its main bank account to its controlled disbursement account;
- Wire transfer from another bank; or
- ACH credit from another bank.

Other methods of funding, including ACH debits or depository transfer checks (DTCs), are much riskier and are rarely used. Each funding method has a different impact on the risk associated with controlled disbursement.

Automated Book Transfer Funding

Typically, with automated book transfer funding, the company's lock box, over-the-counter deposits, and other deposits are concentrated into a single account, which in turn is used to fund an automated book transfer to the controlled disbursement account. The automatic book transfer occurs in the evening, just before final posting. At most banks, the account officer has a significant intraday exposure *information gap*. There is usually no regular internal reporting of morning presentment totals to the account officer, and with money flowing in and out of the customer's various accounts throughout the day, it is not known if covering deposits will be sufficient until they are posted in the evening. The customer could be incurring daylight overdrafts without the account officer's knowledge. Figure 5-2 illustrates the intraday exposure incurred with automatic book transfer funding.

Figure 5-2   Controlled Disbursement Automated Book Transfer Funding

	DAY 0	DAY 1
Intraday Exposure	Bank notified electronically by Fed of total presentments early in morning. Company notified of funding requirement by 10:00 a.m. Company deposits made throughout the day to various transaction accounts. Automated transfers to funding acct and then the controlled disbursement acct. Bank's Fed account is debited for amount of Day 0 presentments.	Account officer becomes aware of overdraft and decides to return checks.

The information gap that allows daylight overdrafts to go unchecked is a characteristic of all zero balance accounts, not just controlled disbursement.

A daylight overdraft can become an overnight overdraft if sufficient funds are not available in time to cover the automatic book transfer in the evening. Nevertheless, the risk can be minimal because there is still ample opportunity to return the checks the next day.

As described above for all check disbursement, the bank would suffer a small loss of the use of funds if it returns the checks. However, if the bank decided not to return the checks, the risk is much greater because the bank could potentially lose the entire amount of the day's presentment.

Wire Transfer Funding

Just as for automated book transfers, an intraday exposure exists with wire transfer funding, but for a shorter duration since the funding wire will be received in the afternoon during banking hours. As we saw for wire transfers in Chapter 4, wires are usually memo posted intraday. If the account officer becomes aware that the funding wire was not received, there is an opportunity to determine the amount of the day's presentment and contact the customer and initiate appropriate action. The extra time compared to automated book transfer funding gives the account officer the opportunity to make a more informed decision regarding possible check returns. The checks could even be returned on the same day if the Operations Department is notified in sufficient time to meet the evening deadline for returns (Figure 5-3).

The loss of use of funds is lower if checks are returned same day instead of next day.

Exposure = (maximum Day 0 presentment) × (1 day) × (cost of funds)

For example, assume the above company's $35,000 check presentment is returned on the same day. Instead of $30.00, the bank's loss will be less than $10.00.

$$(\$35,000) \times (0.1 \times \tfrac{1}{360}) = \$9.72$$

Figure 5-3   Controlled Disbursement Wire Transfer Funding

DAY 0	DAY 1
Bank notified electronically by Fed of total presentments early in morning. Company notified of funding requirement by 10:00 a.m. Afternoon wire deadline. If not received, account officer could decide to return checks. Bank's Fed account is debited for amount of Day 0 presentments.	If checks were not returned Day 0, account officer still has opportunity to return checks.

Intraday Exposure

Obviously, however, the more important benefit from wire transfer funding is the reduction in the duration of the information gap. If the additional time results in a return decision that would not otherwise be made, the bank can potentially avoid a $35,000 loss.

ACH Credit Funding

Funding with an ACH credit that is originated by another bank has similar credit risk as funding with a wire transfer, *plus,* there is a one-day funding lag because ACH is a next day settlement system. An ACH credit originated yesterday is expected to cover checks presented today, so there is a significant risk that the presentment could be underfunded. Most banks reduce the magnitude of the risk by requiring the customer to maintain a prearranged target balance, but there is still a risk that the target balance may not cover all funding shortfalls.

More importantly, there is another risk in receiving ACH credits. All ACH credit entries are provisional and are subject to recall the next day by the Federal Reserve if the originating bank fails. If this occurs, the controlled disbursement bank could miss the next day check return deadline. It would suffer a significant loss if the company subsequently declares bankruptcy and does not provide good funding (Figure 5-4).

Figure 5-4   Controlled Disbursement ACH Credit Funding

DAY 0	DAY 1
Bank receives check presentment.	Fed recalls ACH credit entry.
Bank receives funding ACH credit entry.	
Bank Fed acct debited for presentment.	
Bank Fed acct credited for ACH funding.	Bank Fed account is debited.
Originating bank fails.	

Exposure = (maximum Day 0 presentment) – (target balance)

For example, if the target balance is set at $35,000, but a daily present-ment actually amounts to $45,000, the bank could lose $10,000 if the company fails to fund the shortfall.

($45,000 presentment) – ($35,000 target balance) = $10,000

Without a target balance, the loss to the disbursement bank with ACH credit funding would be the entire $45,000 presentment.

ACH Debit or Depository Transfer Check (DTC) Funding

With this very risky funding method, the controlled disbursement bank would originate an ACH debit or a paper DTC to draw down funds in an account at another bank. Debit funding is very risky because the debit could be returned several days later and well after the check return deadline. In fact, the controlled disbursement bank could be notified of the returned debit after the check return deadline has passed for several more present-ment days (Figure 5-5). The bank could suffer a significant loss unless the target balance was set to cover at least four days' presentments for ACH debit funding and six days' presentments for DTC funding—a precaution certainly not viable in a competitive marketplace.

Exposure = (maximum daily presentment)
     x (maximum number days to return)
     – (target balance)

For example, if as with the ACH credit funding example above, the target balance is set at $35,000, but a daily presentment actually amounts to $45,000, the bank could now lose $145,000 with ACH debit or DTC funding if the return time is assumed to be four days.

($45,000 presentment) x (4 days to return)
  – ($35,000 target balance) = $145,000

Without a target balance, the loss with ACH debit funding would be $180,000.

Figure 5-5   Controlled Disbursement ACH Debit or DTC Funding

DAY 0	DAY 1	DAY2	DAY 2 or 3	DAY 4 , 5 , or 6
Bank initiates ACH or DTC instruction.	Bank makes funds available to company.		Regional banks return debits/DTCs - account frozen.	Bank receives ret'ned debits/DTCs.
Bank delivers debit to ACH or enters DTC in clearing system.	ACH debits/DTCs rec'd by local banks. Bank Fed account is credited.	Company declares bankruptcy.		Bank has unsecured claim against company. Bank Fed account is debited.
		Bank Exposure		

Risk Control Options

Credit risk from controlled disbursement arises from the bank's decision to return, or not return, checks when a customer has insufficient funds on deposit. Control options can improve the bank's quality of information before it makes a return decision. More specifically, they can reduce the duration of the intraday information gap.

Risk control options that reduce the information gap are usually technological in nature, and often expensive to install. They entail making spending decisions that each bank must analyze within the context of its own business environment. Therefore, the first step a bank takes as it moves beyond Stage I informal control should be a well conceived periodic review process. While providing substantially more risk control in its own right, a formal periodic review process also provides the information senior management needs to justify an increased technology investment to support risk control.

Stage II - Periodic Review

As with all other products, periodic review for controlled disbursement facilitates communication between account officers, credit officials, and those responsible for product performance and profitability. The process should force remedial action if specific customers create excessive exposure for the bank.

Figure 5-6 illustrates a monthly report format that combines information about each customer's creditworthiness with the dollar size of its check presentments. The report lists each customer by credit grade, including a category for ungraded customers, and indicates the total dollar amount presented for the month and the dollar size of the largest presentment. The report enables the account officer to examine each customer's recent past exposure, with most attention devoted to low graded and ungraded customers. This usually provides enough time to go back to the customer and negotiate steps to reduce the exposure if necessary. The actions the account officer negotiates with the customer could include a less risky funding alternative, a higher target balance, or some form of collateral, partial collateral or guarantee. It may also mean that the customer should be removed from the service.

The key to periodic review is to have the appropriate plans and procedures in place for effective follow-up. If properly designed, periodic review will provide sufficient control for the vast majority of banks who offer controlled disbursement services.

Stage III - Interactive Control

Interactive control techniques for controlled disbursement can reduce the account officer's intraday information gap by making presentment and funding information available on a more timely basis. It is ironic that even though the main feature of controlled disbursement is timely reporting of presentment totals to the customer early in the day, the vast majority of banks do not automatically make this information available to the account officer. Banks regularly provide customers with more information than their own account officers.

There are two ways to reduce the internal intraday exposure information gap account officers face: provide more timely internal presentment information in the morning and provide more timely funding information in the afternoon.

**Figure 5-6 Monthly Risk Management Report—
Controlled Disbursement**

Account Number	Customer Name	Month X		Month X-1	
		$$ Total Checks	Largest Presentment	$$ Total Checks	Largest Presentment
Credit Grade 9					
. . .					
Credit Grade 8					
. . . .					
Credit Grade 1					
. . . .					
Ungraded					
. . . .					

More timely presentment information. Although it may seem to be an obvious need, very few banks have taken the necessary steps to provide their account officers with morning presentment information. The procedure that provides customers with presentment totals can often be adapted to provide an automated link to update the bank's intraday balance reporting system. This is especially true if customers have the option of receiving controlled disbursement presentment totals electronically through the bank's balance reporting system.

The specific purpose of the automated link would be to enable the bank to automatically hold funds to cover the day's controlled disbursement presentment total. Accounts that have negative intraday balances as a result of the memo posting can be handled in several ways. Controlled disbursement accounts with target balances that have been depleted—those with ACH funding, for instance—may require immediate notification of the account officer. Intraday lines can be established for accounts where funding is expected later in the day with a wire transfer or an automated book transfer. If the presentment debit causes a negative intraday balance that exceeds the intraday line, the account officer should be notified immediately. Likewise, if a transaction later in the day causes the line to be exceeded—a wire transfer, for instance—the account officer can be notified immediately.

Given an automatic warning system, the account officer can contact the customer to determine exactly what is happening and determine if remedial action is necessary. Even without formal lines and automatic notification, the account officer can always access the intraday balance and determine the exact amount of the day's controlled disbursement presentment total if the presentment total automatically updates the intraday balance.

More timely funding information. Funding method is the main determinant of the timeliness of the funding information the account officer receives. We saw earlier in the chapter that wire transfer funding initiated by the customer provides the account officer with funding information much earlier in the day than an automated book transfer from the funding account to the disbursement account. Most banks have a wire deadline around 3:00 p.m., whereas the automated book transfer occurs in the evening at the time the DDA system is posted. Counterbalancing the timing difference, many banks view the book transfer as being less risky because the money is within the bank's system of accounts, whereas the wire moves money from a source totally outside the control of the bank.

A compromise approach is to have the affiliate controlled disbursement bank initiate a drawdown wire transfer by the funding deadline in the afternoon. The funding wire would memo post to the intraday balance just as any other wire transfer. If funds were being held to cover the morning presentment, the hold would be released. If the drawdown wire creates an intraday overdraft, the account officer would be notified immediately.

Check Returns. The bank always has the option to return checks for insufficient funds. All of the risk control options described above ultimately make the account officer's check return decision more informed. If after taking into account all of the information available, the bank does decide to return checks for insufficient funds and eliminate its credit risk, we saw in the risk calculations earlier in the chapter that it will still have a small loss of use of funds because of the way the Federal Reserve accounts for return items.

Although minor, the potential loss can be reduced even further—to approximately one-third—by modifying check processing procedures for known riskier customers. Some banks do this by outsorting the checks of their watch list customers into a separate pocket during check processing in the afternoon. If the account officer decides to return the checks, the operational task would be simplified and same day returns would be possible.

Risk Assessment Worksheet

The Risk Assessment Worksheet in Figure 5-7 can help a bank assess the aggregate controlled disbursement risk it incurs across the customer base and help determine the level of risk control it needs.

Section I of Figure 5-7 summarizes the magnitude of the total potential exposure for the controlled disbursement product line over the past month. The potential exposure is categorized by funding typebook transfer, wire, or ACH funding. The dollar magnitude of the check presentments made to the bank, usually by the Federal Reserve Bank, can be obtained with little difficulty from reports normally produced by the controlled disbursement operations area.

Figure 5-7   Risk Assessment Worksheet—
Controlled Disbursement

I. POTENTIAL EXPOSURE

	Number of Customers	Dollars Presented/Month
Book Transfer Funding	_____	_____
Wire Transfer Funding	_____	_____
ACH Funding	_____	_____
Total	_____	_____

II. CURRENT RISK CONTROLS

(Higher Risk)   (Lower Risk)

Target balances?

☐ None   ☐ Selected accounts   ☐ Many accounts

Formal risk monitoring?

☐ No formal process   ☐ Regular monthly reporting

Are presentments posted to intraday balance in the morning?

☐ No   ☐ Yes

When is the account officer aware that an account is unfunded?

☐ Mid-afternoon   ☐ Late afternoon   ☐ Next morning

Same day check return capability?

☐ No   ☐ Yes

Comments:

_____

_____

III. EXPOSURE AFTER CONTROLS

	Number of Customers	Dollars Presented/Month
Potential Exposure (from Section I.)	_____	_____
Less: customers with target balances	_____	_____
Net Exposure		_____

Figure 5-7 (Continued)

IV. <u>LIKELIHOOD OF LOSS</u>

WATCH LIST CREDIT GRADES

List all watch list customers, except those where exposure has been eliminated with target balances.

<u>Customer Name</u> <u>Dollars Presented/Month</u> <u>Maximum Daily Presentment</u>

| Total Presented/Month | | Percent of Net Exposure | ____% |

MEDIUM CREDIT GRADES

| Total Presented/Month | | Percent of Net Exposure | ____% |

List 5 Largest

HIGHEST CREDIT GRADES

| Total Presented/Month | | Percent of Net Exposure | ____% |

List 3 Largest

UNGRADED CUSTOMERS

| Total Presented/Month | | Percent of Net Exposure | ____% |

List 5 Largest

Figure 5-7 (Continued)

V. OTHER FACTORS

(Higher Risk)   (Lower Risk)

Transaction type?

❏ Vendor and other payments   ❏ Payroll

Volume growth rate?

❏ Rapid growth   ❏ Stable   ❏ Declining

Fraud or operational risks?

❏ High potential   ❏ Low

Comments:

_____

_____

Section II of Figure 5-7 summarizes the risk reduction techniques and risk controls that are currently being used, including target balances, Stage II periodic review, and any Stage III interactive control procedures that reduce the intraday exposure information gap.

Section III of Figure 5-7 calculates the bank's net aggregate exposure after considering the impact of risk reduction and risk controls already in place.

Section IV of Figure 5-7 analyzes the creditworthiness of the remaining customer base to provide an indication of the likelihood that the bank will suffer a loss. The total dollars presented for the month and the largest daily presentment for each customer are categorized by credit grade. Each individual watch list customer is listed with its potential exposure, and customers in the better credit grades with the highest dollar exposure are also individually listed.

Nonborrowing customers are not usually a substantial portion of the controlled disbursement customer base because the product tends to be relationship oriented at many banks. Nevertheless, where nonborrowing customers do exist, their unknown creditworthiness is an important complicating factor. They present serious assessment problems because some could be as risky as those on the watch list. If the number of ungraded customers is too large to allow the individual listing of each customer on the worksheet, list those who create the most exposure.

The difficulty in matching product customer lists with credit grade data in an automated fashion was noted in prior chapters. Even if the task requires a manual effort, accurate matching of information maintained by controlled disbursement operations and credit administration is essential for an effective analysis.

Section V of Figure 5-7 looks at other less tangible factors that should be considered in a complete risk assessment. One example is the impact of the actual application or transaction type. Payroll may be more likely to be funded by a company in a liquidity crisis, for instance, than vendor payments. Another example of a less tangible factor is the growth rate the product has been experiencing. Management might consider rapidly growing controlled disbursement payments to be more risky to the bank than a steady core of payments.

Risk Management Plan

When the risk assessment is completed, the results of the analysis should be the raw material for a comprehensive risk management plan.

Figure 5-8 illustrates the general construct of a sample risk management plan for controlled disbursement. Action plans for each bank will vary considerably, depending upon the bank's level of disbursement activity, technical capability, and credit administration policies. The plan should include approval procedures, required controls, and action steps for customers with deteriorating credit quality.

A system to immediately communicate changes in the status of customers with deteriorating credit is vital. Notification of downgrades should not wait for the next monthly report. In addition to an early notification procedure, contingency action steps should be established for deteriorating credits. The plan should include alternatives to consider and an escalation list of people and phone numbers needed to execute the actions at any time of day or night.

Payable through Drafts

Payable through drafts are payment instruments that look like checks but are actually drawn on the issuing company rather than the bank. The bank acts as clearing agent and conveys the drafts to the issuing company for review and subsequent approval or rejection of payment. The bank will

---

Figure 5-8   **Risk Management Plan—Controlled Disbursement**

Sample Illustration

	Grades 6-9	Grade 5	Grades 1-4
Approval Required	No new customer approvals	Group manager Monthly review	Normal lending authority Annual review
Operation	Alert pocket exception processing. No ACH funding allowed.	Standard No ACH funding allowed.	Standard
Credit Exposure Reduction	Partial target balance for all customers, regardless of funding method.		Target balance for ACH funding.
Credit Exposure	Amount of daily presentment, less partial target balance.	Amount of daily presentment.	Amount of daily presentment, (less target balance, for ACH funding).
Operating Risk	Failure to return checks in timely manner.	Failure to return checks in timely manner.	Failure to return checks in timely manner.

Action Steps for Deteriorating Credit:

1. When the account officer is informed of a downgrading, immediately notify the officer-in-charge of cash management.
2. The account officer and officer-in-charge of cash management will determine action jointly with others as needed (e.g., loan administration, legal, loan workout, operations, etc.). Possible actions include:

    A. A company in a financial crisis can be placed on alert processing on an emergency exception basis to facilitate possible same day check returns should the account officer so decide. The bank's exposure will be limited to the loss of funds for one day.

    B. Negotiate a target balance or a target balance at a higher level.

    C. Negotiate collateral, partial collateral, or guarantee.

    D. Negotiate a combination of target balances and collateral/guarantee.

    Remaining exposure = (max. exposure) - (target balance) - (collateral or guarantee)

    E. Discontinue service if remaining exposure is unacceptable.

3. Cash management will immediately notify operations of actions required.

debit the company's funding account for the amount of the drafts on the day they are presented to the bank.

Payable through drafts give the company time to ensure that all terms have been met (i.e., work was performed, expenditure was authorized, etc.) before payment is approved. The bank usually delivers the drafts to the company for approval during the morning of the day following the bank's receipt of the drafts. The company has until that afternoon to reject any of the drafts and physically return them to the bank, which must subsequently initiate the returns back through the check clearance system before the return deadline in the evening.

As part of their service for selected large volume customers, some banks will maximize the company's time for authorization by receiving presentment information electronically from the Federal Reserve and have the physical drafts delivered directly to the company on the day of presentment. This gives the company an extra day to review and authorize the drafts.

Credit Risk Description

The primary risk associated with payable through drafts is the possibility that the company could fail to fund the drafts presented for payment, either because of bankruptcy or severe liquidity problems. The risk for payable through drafts is identical to the risk for all check disbursement services as outlined in Figure 5-1.

Regulation CC defines a payable through draft as a check and requires a "payable through" bank to perform all the functions and duties of a "paying" bank. Therefore, should a company not fund its drafts, the bank is permitted to return the drafts on the business day following presentment.

Even if drafts are returned, the bank always incurs a small loss of its use of funds. The Federal Reserve always debits the bank's Federal Reserve account on the day the checks are presented for payment. If the bank decides to return the checks the following day, the Federal Reserve will recredit the bank's account the day after it receives the returns—two days after the original presentment debit. The bank loses the use of those funds for two days.

Customer Risk Calculation

The maximum exposure due to this loss of the use of funds is calculated as follows if the bank decides to return the drafts.

$$\text{Exposure} = (\text{ maximum Day 0 presentment }) \times (\text{ 2 days }) \times (\text{ cost of funds })$$
$$+$$
$$(\text{ maximum Day 1 presentment }) \times (\text{ cost of funds })$$

For example, assume that a company's drafts are presented for payment every day, with a history of daily presentment amounts that are no greater than $50,000. If the company fails to fund the drafts, and the bank decides to return the checks, the bank will still incur a very small loss. If the bank's cost of funds is 10%, the loss will be about $40.00.

$$(\ \$50,000\ ) \times (\text{ 2 days }) \times (\ 0.1 \times \tfrac{1}{360}\ ) = \$27.77$$
$$(\ \$50,000\ ) \times (\ 0.1 \times \tfrac{1}{360}\ ) = \quad 13.89$$

$$\overline{}$$
$$\$41.66$$

However, if the bank decided to extend credit and pay the drafts, the bank could lose the entire $50,000 if the company subsequently declared bankruptcy.

Just as with controlled disbursement, there are additional risks associated with the specific funding method used. The same risks associated with each funding option associated with controlled disbursement apply to payable through drafts, so they will not be repeated here.

Special note should be made, however, that even though ACH debit and paper depository transfer check (DTC) funding is extremely risky and should be strongly discouraged, some banks surprisingly allow customers to fund payable through drafts with DTCs. This is most likely a holdover from earlier practice, when DTCs and payable through drafts were much more commonly used, and before operating credit risk was the concern it is today. DTC funding is not as likely to be discouraged as other risky activity because payable through draft volume is declining at most banks in favor of electronic alternatives, and the practice often escapes the scrutiny of risk managers concerned with more visible and growing product lines.

The maximum exposure a bank has to a customer that funds payable through drafts with DTCs can be very large because the DTC can be returned several days later—after the draft return deadline, and after several more draft presentments have been made. The maximum exposure is illustrated in Figure 5-9 and is calculated as follows:

$$\text{Exposure} = (\text{maximum daily presentment})$$
$$\times (\text{maximum number days to return})$$

For example, if the maximum daily presentment is $75,000, the bank could have an exposure of $225,000. This assumes three days to return the funding DTCs. The return time usually takes longer than three days for most paper items, but Federal Reserve Regulation CC requires that the paying bank must notify the depository bank by 4:00 p.m. of the second business day following presentment if it decides to return a check of $2,500 or more. Most funding DTCs exceed the $2,500 threshold.

Figure 5-9   **Payable through Drafts DTC Funding**

DAY 0	DAY 1	DAY 2	DAY 3	DAY 4 or 5
Bank receives draft presentment.	Bank receives Day 1 draft presentment.	Bank receives Day 2 draft presentment.	Funding bank notifies bank that DTC is being returned--account frozen.	Bank receives returned DTC.
Bank enters DTC in check clearing system.	Day 0 DTC received by funding bank.			Bank has unsecured claim against company.
	Bank Fed account is credited.	Company declares bankruptcy.	Bank returns drafts not past deadline.	Bank Fed account is debited.
		Bank Exposure		

Risk Control Options

The most important risk control option for payable through drafts is to ensure that the bank has been funded with good and immediately available funds on the day of presentment. All of the options described above for controlled disbursement apply because they provide the account officer with as much information as possible to facilitate the return decision if the customer has insufficient funds to cover the presentment.

If the bank establishes a policy that the customer must have good funds on deposit on the day of presentment, the bank should also indicate that the funding is provisional. Since the company will review and may reject some portion of the drafts, the bank will be obligated to refund the funding for rejected drafts.

Figure 5-7, the risk assessment worksheet for controlled disbursement, can be easily adapted for payable through drafts.

Risk Management Plan

Figure 5-10 illustrates the general outline of sample risk management plan for payable through drafts. Each bank should carefully construct its own plan based upon its own risk assessment and its own trade-offs between potential loss and the cost of various risk control options. The most important point is that the results of a thorough risk assessment should be documented and enforced.

Correspondent Bank Cash Letters

Some banks allow their Federal Reserve accounts to be used by correspondent banks to settle checks drawn on the correspondent. The bank offering this service typically receives the correspondents' in-clearings from the Federal Reserve Bank in the morning, sorts the checks by bank, and transmits the MICR line information to each respective correspondent bank or its service bureau. The bank then either delivers the physical checks to the correspondent, and the correspondent is then responsible for any subsequent returns; or safekeeps the physical checks and prepares the daily return item cash letter for the correspondent.

Credit Risk Description

The credit risk of the bank offering the service to the correspondent depends upon whether or not the service includes safekeeping.

Figure 5-10   Risk Management Plan—Payable through Drafts

Sample Illustration

	Grades 6-9	Grade 5	Grades 1-4
Approval Required	No new customer approvals.	Group manager Monthly review	Normal lending authority Annual review
Operation	Wire transfer funding only.	Standard No ACH or DTC funding allowed.	Standard No DTC funding allowed.
Credit Exposure Reduction	Partial target balance for all customers, regardless of funding method.		Target balance for ACH funding.
Credit Exposure	None (unless decision is made not to return unfunded drafts).	Amount of daily presentment (if drafts are not returned).	Amount of daily presentment, (less target balance, for ACH funding) .
Operating Risk	Failure to return drafts in timely manner.	Failure to return drafts in timely manner .	Failure to return drafts in timely manner .

Action Steps for Deteriorating Credit:

1. When the account officer is informed of a downgrading, immediately notify the officer-in-charge of cash management.

2. The account officer and officer-in-charge of cash management will determine action jointly with others as needed (e.g., loan administration, legal, loan workout, operations, etc.). Possible actions include:
   - A. Negotiate wire transfer funding.
   - B. Negotiate a target balance for non-wire funding.
   - C. Negotiate collateral, partial collateral, or guarantee.

   Remaining exposure = (max. exposure) - (target balance/collateral/guarantee)
   - D. Discontinue service if remaining exposure is unacceptable.

3. Cash management will immediately notify operations of actions required.

With Safekeeping

The bank's credit risk is small because the bank has physical possession of the checks and the ability to return them if the correspondent has insufficient funds in its account with the bank. The bank's right to return checks in an overdraft situation, even though they are drawn on the correspondent, is usually part of the written service agreement.

If there is an overdraft, and the bank decides to return checks, there is still a loss of use of funds because the Federal Reserve's credit for returns would not occur until the following day—and the credit is not back-valued. The mechanics are the same as those described for check disbursement in Figure 5-1, but since the total dollars cleared can be quite large, the loss of use of funds is more significant than it was in the prior check disbursement examples. If the bank returns the checks drawn on the correspondent on the same day they are presented, its loss of use of funds would be calculated as follows:

$$\text{Exposure} = (\text{maximum Day 0 presentment}) \times (2 \text{ days}) \times (\text{cost of funds})$$

For example, if the maximum expected daily presentment is $10,000,000, and the bank's cost of funds is 10%, the bank could lose over $2,700.

$$(\$10,000,000) \times (0.1 \times \tfrac{1}{360}) = \$2,777.78$$

If checks are returned next day, the calculation is as follows:

$$\text{Exposure} = (\text{maximum Day 0 presentment}) \times (2 \text{ days}) \times (\text{cost of funds})$$
$$+$$
$$(\text{maximum Day 1 presentment}) \times (\text{cost of funds})$$

Using the same assumptions, the bank would then lose over $8,000.

$$(\$10,000,000) \times (2 \text{ days}) \times (0.1 \times \tfrac{1}{360}) = \$5,555.56$$
$$(\$10,000,000) \times (0.1 \times \tfrac{1}{360}) = 2,777.78$$

$$\overline{ \$8,333.34}$$

As with all check disbursements, the decision to return checks is a credit decision. Even with the physical checks in the possession of the bank, the decision could be made to not return checks. In that event, the entire overdraft is at risk—potentially the entire $10,000,000 presentment.

Without Safekeeping

Without safekeeping, the risk is much greater because the bank's return option does not exist. If the correspondent fails, the entire amount of the overdraft is exposed, and potentially the entire day's presentment—$10,000,000 in the above example.

Recent history indicates that when a thrift is taken over by the Resolution Trust Corporation (RTC), the RTC will generally cover the overdraft. The risk is sometimes greater when an institution is taken over by the FDIC, which some banks have found is less likely to cover the overdraft.

Check Collection

Check collection services comprise many of the most widely used operating services banks provide to both corporate and correspondent bank customers. They typically include wholesale and retail lock box, over-the-counter, and other deposit services for corporate customers and cash letter deposit services for correspondent banks. They all represent various forms of customer check deposits that the bank needs to clear and make available to the customer for withdrawal.

Wholesale Lock Box

All lock box services are designed to expedite the conversion of incoming mailed payments into funds that can be used by a company. Lock box services reduce the float caused by mail delivery, remittance processing, and check collection time. Lock box services also eliminate many of the clerical expenses companies incur when they process their own remittances.

Wholesale lock box is the most widely used and simplest service available to help a company accelerate the collection of remittances through the mail. The service consists of a post office box in the company's name, to which the bank alone has access. The bank picks up the remittances several times a day, credits funds to the company's account, and forwards the invoices and any other materials received to the company. Wholesale lock box is typically used for high dollar, low volume, corporate-to-corporate remittances. The company is notified of daily deposits via the bank's electronic balance reporting service, telephone, or facsimile transmission. The service enables a company to more rapidly use its remittance cash flow to pay down loans, make short-term investments, or take advantage of cash discounts on trade payables.

Retail Lock Box

Retail lock box is usually a highly automated service that is designed for customers who receive a large volume of small dollar remittances by mail on a daily basis. The service utilizes the latest technological developments in optical character recognition (OCR) or image processing equipment to capture remittance information and convert it directly to computer readable form. Remittance information is usually transmitted to the customer's accounts receivable system, either directly by the bank using its own technology, or alternatively, through a third-party vendor. The service allows companies to develop highly efficient automated receivables systems that can be posted same day.

Over-the-Counter Services

Over-the-counter services include deposits of check payments at bank branches during regular banking hours, as well as a great variety of specialized deposit services for high dollar or high volume deposits. Many banks offer specialized corporate check deposit services where customers can deliver checks directly to the bank's operations center or branch locations during night-time hours. They offer a variety of priced services to more rapidly convert remittances to usable funds, depending upon the time of the deposit, the volume of checks, whether the checks are pre-encoded or unencoded, and other service parameters.

Correspondent Bank Cash Letters

Sometimes banks with significant check processing capabilities offer cash letter services to correspondent banks. The service provides correspondent banks with a "direct send" alternative to using Federal Reserve or other private check clearance services to process their check deposits. Banks offering these deposit clearing services usually have a variety of programs from which the correspondent can choose. Typical examples include same clearing house cash letters, mixed cash letters, and "on-us" cash letters.

Same clearing house cash letters. Correspondent banks can direct send deposits of pre-encoded checks drawn on any bank that is a member of the same clearing house as the bank offering the service. The bank offering the service attracts volume because it is able to provide correspondents with better availability than normal Federal Reserve processing.

Mixed cash letters. Because the bank offering the service likely has an efficient network of direct send arrangements it makes to clear its own deposits, it is able to accept correspondent cash letters with checks drawn on any bank in the United States and provide a competitive service. It may also provide encoding services and accept either pre-encoded or unencoded checks.

"On-us" cash letters. The bank may offer immediate availability for pre-encoded checks drawn on the bank if received by a stated deadline.

There are many other possible combinations for cash letter services. Pricing is usually time or deadline sensitive, with varying combinations of float pricing and per item pricing.

Credit Risk Description

After receiving a check deposit, the bank gives the company (or correspondent) ledger credit on its books and determines when the deposit will become available to the company (or correspondent) for withdrawal. The availability the bank assigns to a company is constrained by Federal Reserve Regulation CC. In many banks, availability is part of the pricing for check collection services, and it varies depending upon the service provided.

The primary risk associated with all check collection services is the possibility that checks could be returned after the bank makes funds available to the company, and after the company has withdrawn the funds. This happens quite often, but it is normally not a serious problem because banks routinely charge back the amount of the returned checks to the company's account. In the event of bankruptcy, however, the company's account could be frozen by the court or it may not have sufficient balances to cover the charge-back for returns. This sequence of events is illustrated in Figure 5-11.

The risk is complicated somewhat by Federal Reserve Regulation CC: Availability of Funds and Collection of Checks. Figure 5-12 outlines the salient points of Regulation CC as it impacts the credit risk associated with

Figure 5-11   Check Collection

DAY 0	DAY 1/3	DAY 2/4	DAY 3/6
Deposit to company (or correspondent) account.	Bank makes funds available to company. (Exact day depends on availability assigned).	Payor banks initiate individual check returns.	Bank receives returned checks.
Bank provides ledger credit to company.	Bank Fed or other clearance account is credited.	Company declares bankruptcy.	Bank Fed or other clearance account is debited.
Bank initiates check clearance process and assigns availability to company.		Company account at bank is frozen by court.	Bank has unsecured claim against company.
	Bank Exposure		

check collection. Local checks must be made available for withdrawal "not later than the second business day following the banking day on which the checks were deposited." Nonlocal checks must be made available for withdrawal "not later than the fifth business day following deposit."

Credit risk arises because the actual collection and return process is not always completed within the time allowed by Regulation CC. If a deposit is made on Monday, local funds must be made available by Wednesday, and nonlocal funds must be made available within five banking days, on the following Monday. However, Figure 5-12 shows that for checks processed by the Federal Reserve, the bank of first deposit will likely receive a local return on Friday, a full two days after funds were made available for withdrawal on Wednesday. Likewise, a nonlocal return will likely be received on Tuesday, one day after funds were made available.

This timing problem will gradually diminish as the technology for return item processing improves. Figure 5-12 only illustrates the Federal Reserve collection and return process. The timing varies with private proc-

Figure 5-12   Availability/Collectibility

Federal Reserve Regulation CC Availability

Mon	Tue	Wed	Thur	Fri	Mon	Tue
Deposit		Local Funds Available			Non-Local Funds Available	

Federal Reserve Collection/Return Process

Mon	Tue	Wed	Thur	Fri	Mon	Tue
Deposit	Presentment to Payor	Payor Initiates Return	Large $ Notification	Local Return Received by BOFD		Non-Local Rtrn. Rec'd by BOFD

BOFD=Bank of first deposit

essors, and private sector alternatives are being examined by an increasing number of banks. Besides well established direct send arrangements and the use of the local clearing houses, two nationwide clearing houses have been formed—National Clearing House and Electronic Check Clearing House Organization (Eccho).

Customer Risk Calculation

Corporate Deposits

The maximum credit exposure a bank has to a corporate customer that deposits checks depends upon the return rate that can be expected, as well as the number of days it takes to receive a return.

Exposure = (maximum daily deposit) × (maximum days return)
× (return rate)

For example, assume that a company has daily lock box deposits that range up to $30,000/day. Its historic check return rate has been about 3%. If the company declares bankruptcy and is unable to cover the charge-backs by the bank for the returned checks, the bank could lose $4,500.

($30,000) × (5 days to return) × (0.03 return rate) = $4,500

Even though five days were assumed, the bank in this example does not regularly track how long it takes to receive a returned check. Regulation CC details the paying bank's responsibility for the return of checks (Appendix C). In general, those responsibilities are as follows:

- The paying bank must deposit a check for forward collection by noon on the banking day following presentment.
- Alternatively, the paying bank must return a check so that it would normally be received by the depository bank by 4:00 p.m. of the: (a) second business day following presentment in the same check processing region; or (b) fourth business day if not in the same check processing region.
- The paying bank must also notify the depository bank by 4:00 p.m. of the second business day following presentment if it decides to return a check of $2,500 or more.

Based on the above, the number of days to return a check can vary substantially, depending upon the location of the paying bank or the size of the check. Return times are also impacted by weather and transportation problems. Ideally, return time estimates should be based on the bank's actual customer and product histories. Absent actual histories, assume at least five days are needed for check collection—one day to initiate the return, plus four days for nonlocal returns to be received.

Correspondent Cash Letter Deposits

The calculation for correspondent check deposits is the same as the calculation for companies, but special note is made because correspondent deposits are often very large. For example, a $3 million deposit with five days to return and a 3% return rate could result in a $450,000 loss if the correspondent bank was unable to cover the charge-back for returns.

($3,000,000) × (5 days to return) × (0.03 return rate) = $450,000

Risk Assessment Worksheet

The Risk Assessment Worksheet in Figure 5-13 is specifically designed for lock box, but it can be readily adapted to other check collection services. It is intended to help a bank assess the aggregate return item risk it incurs across the lock box customer base. In addition, it provides a checklist to help the bank focus on the most important risk factors.

Section I of Figure 5-13 summarizes the total potential exposure from lock box returns over the past month. The dollar amounts of lock box deposits by customer can usually be obtained with little difficulty from reports produced by the lock box operations area. Return statistics by customer may be more difficult to obtain.

Section II of Figure 5-13 summarizes the risk reduction techniques and risk controls that are currently being used—primarily collateral, guarantees, and Stage II periodic review procedures.

Section III of Figure 5-13 calculates the bank's net aggregate exposure after considering the impact of risk reduction and risk controls in place.

Section IV of Figure 5-13 analyzes the creditworthiness of the remaining customer base to provide an indication of the likelihood that the bank will suffer a loss. Total deposits for each customer are categorized by credit grade, along with the total returns for each customer. Individual watch list customers are listed with their potential exposure, and customers in the better credit grades with the highest dollar exposure are also individually listed.

The unknown creditworthiness of nonborrowing customers is important to consider because some could be as risky as those on the watch list. If the number of ungraded customers is too large to allow the individual listing of each customer on the worksheet, list those who create the most exposure.

Section V of Figure 5-13 looks at other less tangible factors that should be considered in a complete risk assessment. For example, the transaction type and its importance to the consumer is an important factor to consider when assessing the likelihood of returns. A consumer is more likely to make sure good funds are available for a rent payment than a magazine subscription.

Figure 5-13   Risk Assessment Worksheet—Lock Box

I. POTENTIAL EXPOSURE

Number of Customers: _____

Dollars Deposited/Month: _____

Dollars Returned/Month: _____

II. CURRENT RISK CONTROLS

(Higher Risk)   (Lower Risk)

Collateral or guarantees?

☐ None   ☐ Selected accounts

Formal risk monitoring?

☐ No formal process   ☐ Regular monthly
                                              reporting

Comments:

_____
_____
_____
_____
_____

III. EXPOSURE AFTER CONTROLS

	No. Customers	$ Deposited/Mo.	$ Returned/Mo.
Potential Exposure (from Section I.)	_____	_____	_____
Less: customers with collateral	_____	_____	_____
Less: customers with guarantees	_____	_____	_____

Net (Return) Exposure   _____

Figure 5-13 (Continued)

IV. LIKELIHOOD OF LOSS

WATCH LIST CREDIT GRADES

List all watch list customers, except those where exposure has been eliminated with collateral or guarantees.

Customer Name	Dollars Deposited/Month	Dollars Returned/Month

| Total Returned/Month | _____ | Percent of Net Exposure | ____% |

MEDIUM CREDIT GRADES

| Total Returned/Month | _____ | Percent of Net Exposure | ____% |

List 5 Largest

HIGHEST CREDIT GRADES

| Total Returned/Month | _____ | Percent of Net Exposure | ____% |

List 3 Largest

UNGRADED CUSTOMERS

| Total Returned/Month | _____ | Percent of Net Exposure | ____% |

List 5 Largest

Figure 5-13 (Continued)

V. <u>OTHER FACTORS</u>

(Higher Risk)   (Lower Risk)

Importance to Consumer (TransactionType)?

    ❑ Mostly less important   ❑ Mixed   ❑ Mostly more important
        e.g. , magazine subscription   e.g. , rent payment

Volume growth rate?

    ❑ Rapid growth   ❑ Stable

Fraud or operational risks?

    ❑ High potential   ❑ Low

Comments:

Risk Control Options

Although less obviously applicable, it is still useful to look at credit risk control for check collection in the context of the stages of risk control evolution: Should exposures be prevented before they occur, or is it sufficient to monitor exposures after the fact?

Stage II – Periodic Review

Periodic review is the most appropriate form of risk control in the vast majority of check collection customers because return exposures are usually relatively small compared to other credit exposures, and Stage III – Interactive Control options are quite limited for check collection.

    An interesting side note to lock box is the fact that some banks use the lock box product itself as an overall credit risk monitoring tool. They *require* their watch list credit customers to use the bank for any lock box activity they may have. By tracking lock box usage, they feel that they have a better handle on that customer's shaky financial situation.

    The backbone of an effective periodic review process is a regular monthly report that indicates the dollar exposure of each customer—especially in the riskier watch list credit grades. Figure 5-14 illustrates an effective format. The total deposits, total returns, and the return rate is listed

Figure 5-14   Monthly Risk Management Report—Lock Box

		Month X			Month X-1		
Account Number	Customer Name	$$ Total Deposits	Total Returns	Rate	$$ Total Deposits	Total Returns	Rate
Credit Grade 9							
·							
·							
·							
Credit Grade 8							
·							
·							
·							
·							
Credit Grade 1							
·							
·							
·							
·							
·							
·							
·							
Ungraded							
·							
·							
·							
·							

for each customer in credit grade categories and for ungraded customers. Some may prefer to only list watch list and ungraded customers.

Stage III – Interactive Control

Maintaining separate check availability and collectibility schedules can enable a bank to exercise a level of interactive control over check collection credit exposures. An availability schedule indicates the number of days a customer must wait before a check deposit is available for withdrawal. The risk to the bank is that a deposited check could be returned after the funds have been withdrawn by the customer. Weaker customers may not have sufficient funds to cover the bank's chargeback.

A collectibility schedule indicates the number of days after deposit the bank can no longer expect returns. Some banks, therefore, place riskier customers on a collectibility schedule.

Regulation CC severely limits this option but does not prevent it entirely. Exceptions to the required availability schedule can be made for new accounts, deposits in excess of $5,000, redeposited checks, repeated overdrafts, reasonable cause to doubt collectibility, and emergency conditions. Reasonable cause to doubt collectibility can include the reasonable belief that the depositor is engaging in kiting activity. Regulation CC also requires that when a depository bank extends availability based on allowable exceptions, it must provide the depositor with a written notice that includes the account number, the date and amount of the deposit, the portion of the deposit that is being delayed, the reason for the delay, and the day the funds will be available.

Details regarding exceptions and notification requirements are found in the Regulation CC excerpts in Appendix C.

Risk Management Plan

Figure 5-15 illustrates the general construct of a sample risk management plan for lock box. A similar approach can be used for other check collection services. The plan could vary considerably for each bank, depending upon the bank's policy toward having riskier customers use lock box and the bank's technical capability for maintaining multiple availability schedules. Each bank should carefully construct its own plan based upon its own risk assessment and its own analysis of trade-offs between potential losses and the benefits of providing lock box services.

Figure 5-15   Risk Management Plan—Lock Box

Sample Illustration

	Grades 6-9	Grade 5	Grades 1-4
Approval Required	Group manager Monthly review	Group manager Monthly review	Normal lending authority Annual review
Operation	Consider delaying availability per Reg CC.	Standard	Standard
Credit Exposure Reduction	Consider collateral or guarantee for returns.		
Credit Exposure	Returns, less collateral or guarantee.	All returns	All returns
Operating Risk			

Action Steps for Deteriorating Credit:

1. When the account officer is informed of a downgrading, immediately notify the officer-in-charge of cash management.
2. The account officer and officer-in-charge of cash management will determine action jointly with others as needed (e.g., loan administration, legal, loan workout, operations, etc.). Possible actions include:
   A. Delay availability within the constraints of Regulation CC.
   B. Negotiate collateral, partial collateral, or guarantee.
   C Discontinue service.
3. Cash management will immediately notify operations of actions required.

Figure 5-16   **Outgoing Cash Letter**

Day 0	Day 1/2/3	Day 2/3/4
	Corres. credits bank's acct. and grants bank availability.	Bank charges back individual depositors. Some unable to cover chargeback.
Bank receives deposits from individual depositors.	Bank gives individual depositors availability.	
Bank direct sends to Correspondent.	Corres. fails. Bank has unsecured claim as uninsured depositor.	

Outgoing Cash Letters

In addition to the return risk described above, there is another credit risk associated with check collection services—the method a bank chooses to process check deposits for collection.

Direct sending of outgoing cash letters to correspondent banks creates more credit risk than using the Federal Reserve System because the sending bank receives availability from the correspondent, and in turn passes availability to its depositors. If the correspondent fails and does not settle the checks, the bank sending the cash letter will have an unsecured claim as an uninsured depositor. In that situation, the bank will charge back each of the original depositor accounts. There is a risk that some of the individual depositors will not have sufficient funds to cover the charge-backs. Figure 5-16 illustrates a possible time sequence of events. In most cases, the risk to the bank is minimal, but it is possible that charge-backs could adversely impact certain depositors on shaky financial ground.

6

SECURITIES SERVICES

Banks offer corporate securities services to a broad range of institutional investors, including brokerage houses, insurance companies, investment managers, and pension funds. For some banks, custody and safekeeping services are a major contributor to fee-based earnings. However, as with most operating services, securities services incur operating credit risk.

When acting as custodial agent on behalf of its customers, the bank's function is to receive or deliver securities and make or receive payments according to the instructions of the customer. The bank also collects and credits dividend, interest, and other income payments in accordance with instructions. Since the bank does not usually have discretionary authority, it is totally dependent on the instructions of the customer. Legally, it acts as the customer's agent when executing securities transactions on behalf of the customer.

The intraday credit exposure created by securities transactions is of particular concern. Credit exposure most commonly exists when securities are received into the customer's account, especially when the customer is in a deficit position. To a lesser extent, there can also be exposure in some situations when the bank delivers securities from the customer's custody or safekeeping account to the customer's counterparty.

Receiving Transactions

Extension of intraday credit is common practice when custody banks receive securities into customer accounts. Acting upon the customer's instruction, the bank will often execute payments before the customer provides sufficient funds in the associated cash account. The bank assumes a credit risk because good funds may not arrive later in the day when they are expected.

In Figure 6-1, the customer instructs the bank to advance payment for specific securities the bank will receive. When the securities arrive, the bank credits them to the customer's account and advances funds for the securities received. The bank will debit the customer's cash account for the value advanced, although there may not be sufficient funds in the account to cover the transaction. Under normal circumstances, the customer will provide sufficient good funds to cover the overdraft before the day is over.

However, if the company unexpectedly develops severe financial difficulties or declares bankruptcy before the cash account is sufficiently funded, the routine intraday overdraft could become an overnight overdraft, or more importantly, an actual loss for the bank.

Figure 6-1   Securities Received

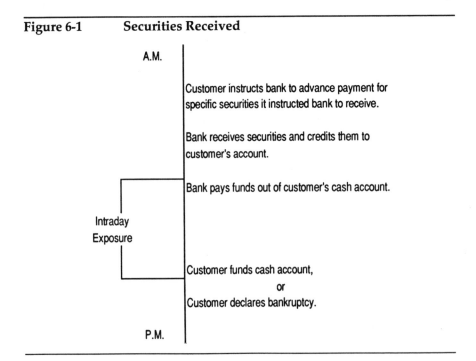

A.M.

Customer instructs bank to advance payment for specific securities it instructed bank to receive.

Bank receives securities and credits them to customer's account.

Bank pays funds out of customer's cash account.

Intraday Exposure

Customer funds cash account,

or

Customer declares bankruptcy.

P.M.

Risk Control Options

The bank will often make the payment for securities received using a wire transfer, or another immediately available payment method. Likewise, the bank will generally receive cover from the customer later in the day via wire transfer as well. Therefore, many of the risk control options available for securities received are similar to those for wire transfer. We saw in Chapter 4 that the Federal Reserve's self-assessment guide contains an important section on monitoring intraday customer positions and includes an extensive checklist of factors to consider (Appendix A).

The checklist can help the bank decide to what degree interactive controls are necessary in relation to the daylight overdrafts associated with securities transactions. The most important characteristic of interactive control is that it gives the bank the ability to prevent unwanted daylight overdraft exposure before it occurs, whereas periodic review notifies management of exposures after they have already occurred.

Stage II - Periodic Review

An appropriately designed periodic review process will provide the information senior management needs to determine if interactive control is necessary for securities-related wire transfers. Because of the high dollar nature of securities deliveries, these wire transfers can comprise a significant portion of overall wire transfer risk at many banks.

The sample report in Figure 4-14 indicates the largest users of wire transfer for management review. The report is produced on a monthly basis in this example, and it highlights the total dollars wired out for each customer for the month and the amount of the largest wire. Most importantly, customers are categorized by credit grade to give management a perspective on the actual level of customer credit risk involved. Depending on the actual customers involved, the report could easily be produced at more frequent intervals if management deemed it necessary for watch list customers in riskier credit grades.

Stage III - Interactive Controls

Banks with interactive controls for daylight overdrafts require the wire transfer department to check the customer's balance and place a hold on the account before an outgoing wire is completed. "Funds control" systems can range from totally manual procedures to highly automated. Regardless of the degree of automation, if the customer's account does not have sufficient balances to cover the wire request, the account officer is contacted for approval before the wire is released.

If these interactive procedures result in a burdensome number of account officer referrals, intraday credit limits can also be established for creditworthy customers. With intraday limits, the account officer is contacted for approval only if the available balance plus the intraday limit is insufficient to cover the wire request. The sample periodic report in Figure 4-15 includes columns for each customer's assigned daylight overdraft limit and the number of times the customer's wire request exceeded the limit and required credit referral. Daylight overdraft limits must be reviewed on a regular basis, and customers that are frequently referred for credit approval require special attention to determine if the limit is still appropriate.

With or without credit limits, it is important for the account officer to understand all of the customer's expected activity, whether securities related or not, before outgoing wires are approved. Few bank funds control systems capture all transactions online. The feeder systems and the resulting intraday balance may not reflect an important large transaction that the account officer should be expecting.

Customer Risk Calculation

Even with a highly automated funds control system, the exposure to a specific customer depends on the accuracy of the intraday balance at the time of the credit referral and approval.

$$Exposure = (\text{intraday limit})$$
$$+$$
$$(\text{overlimit approvals})$$
$$+$$
$$(\text{significant debit transactions that are not memo posted intraday})$$

If the bank does not use preapproved intraday credit limits, the calculation is similar.

$$Exposure = (\text{intraday overdraft approvals})$$
$$+$$
$$(\text{significant debit transactions that are not memo posted intraday})$$

Risk Management Plan

The risk assessment worksheet and risk management plan presented in relation to wire transfers in Chapter 4 are applicable to wire transfers associated with securities services, as is the Federal Reserve's checklist for monitoring customer positions in Appendix A. Each bank should carefully construct its own plan based upon its risk assessment and an analysis of trade-offs between potential loss and the cost of various levels of control.

The actual risk associated with securities received transactions also depends upon whether the customer holds its own assets in safekeeping with the bank, or holds assets in a fiduciary capacity on behalf of its customers.

Lien on Customer Assets

When the bank holds the customer's own assets in safekeeping, most legal agreements between the bank and the customer provide an additional level of protection in the form of a lien upon the securities held in safekeeping. However, no matter how strongly the lien is worded, it is only effective if the customer has assets of sufficient quality and quantity to cover the bank's exposure.

Collateral or Guarantees

An option that can be considered for customers with unacceptable intraday exposure, and insufficient securities held in safekeeping to cover the exposure, is to negotiate an arrangement whereby the customer purchases interest-bearing certificates of deposit and pledges them back to the bank to cover the exposure.

Nevertheless, there is always the possibility that the size of the securities transaction could exceed the amount collateralized or guaranteed. Nevertheless, collateral or guarantees provide a large measure of protection and should be considered a serious alternative.

Competitive pressure is the most difficult obstacle. Requiring collateral, or even partial collateral, may make sense from a risk perspective, but the option is severely limited if competitors are willing to provide the service without that protection. In some cases, the only viable option is to not offer the service to customers if their credit quality is too risky.

Fiduciary Assets

Exposure issues can be more serious when the bank's customer holds assets in a fiduciary capacity on behalf of its own customers. In that case, the bank is legally precluded from holding a lien against the securities held in safekeeping because the customer does not own the securities.

One way to reduce the bank's exposure when the customer is a fiduciary is to establish by agreement that securities received are not the control of the customer until they have been fully paid for by the customer. The agreement should clearly establish that until the bank receives good funds, the bank should have rights to the securities as the party advancing the funds. It is extremely important that the bank's legal counsel reviews all custody and safekeeping agreements to ensure adequate protection for the bank.

Delivery Transactions

Upon customer instructions, banks also deliver securities to the customer's counterparties for payment. Because delivery and payment are not simultaneous occurrences, the bank's customer has an intraday period of risk associated with each delivery transaction.

In Figure 6-2, the customer instructs the bank to deliver securities to a counterparty and expect payment later in the day. When the securities are delivered to the counterparty, it is possible that the counterparty may, in turn, redeliver the securities to another party. Under normal circumstances, the counterparty will make the payment later in the day as expected.

There is a risk that the payment may never arrive from the counterparty. If this occurs, the customer has the primary risk and the bank would normally reverse the debit to the customer's account for the amount of the securities delivered. However, the bank incurs a risk that the customer could declare bankruptcy before the reversal. The bank could suffer a loss if the securities are unrecoverable from the counterparty—for instance if bearer securities were redelivered to another party by the counterparty.

Risk Control Options

If the bank knows in advance of the insolvency of the customer's counterparty, one way for the bank to protect itself from this kind of delivery exposure is to require a letter from the customer acknowledging the insolvency of the counterparty. The letter should authorize the delivery of the

Figure 6-2   Securities Delivery

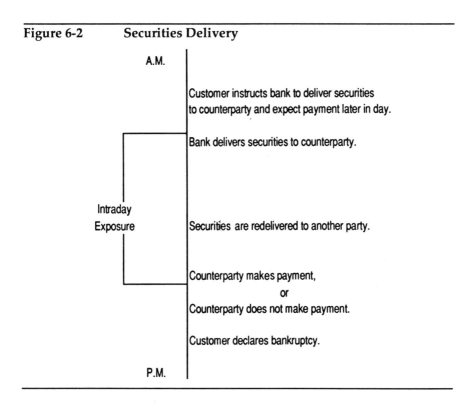

securities and state that the customer accepts the risk of nonpayment if the counterparty defaults. Figure 6-3 illustrates a sample letter that can be used to help protect the bank.

The overall custody agreement with the customer and related letters like the sample shown can place clear financial responsibility on the customer for the consequences of dealing with an insolvent counterparty. Nevertheless, if the customer were to face such a loss, the bank is still dependent upon the financial ability of the customer to successfully absorb the loss. There are no interactive operating controls that can substitute for close credit scrutiny of all of the bank's custody and safekeeping customers.

Figure 6-3   Sample Letter—Securities Delivery

Investment Company
(Customer Letterhead)

<Date>

```
<Bank Officer>
<Bank Name>
<Bank Address>

Dear <Bank Officer>:

This is authorization for <Bank Name> to deliver all
<Security Name> transactions to <Insolvent Company> as
instructed.

We are aware that <Insolvent Company> has filed for
bankruptcy and we accept all risk of non payment.

                    Sincerely,


                    Authorized Signature
```

Other Exposures

Income Availability to Customer

In addition to the intraday exposures described for receive and delivery transactions, exposures are created by bank guarantees of availability of income funds to the customer in a competitive market. Depending upon the market in which it operates, the bank often has to negotiate a guaranteed date for crediting dividend and interest income to the customer's custody account. This is especially true for the large banks who provide global custody services.

To be competitive, many of the banks who offer custodial services guarantee to sweep all dividend and interest payments into the customer's account on the day payment is due, or some other guaranteed date very close to the due date, regardless of the time the payments actually arrive. If interest or dividend payments arrive after the guaranteed date, the bank will lose the investment value of those payments for the period they are late. Conversely, if interest or dividend payments arrive before the guaranteed date, the bank will gain.

Group of Thirty Recommendation

Banks often provide cash management services to their customers in the investment community, including brokerage houses and other securities firms, who in turn provide retail securities services to a large consumer customer base. Banks offer securities firms a complete array of check and ACH-based services to collect funds from retail customers. Most of the risk issues are the same as those discussed in Chapters 4 and 5, but there are specific concerns associated with ACH that deserve further attention.

The timing of securities payments has been an important consideration for the Group of Thirty, and their recommendations have received a great deal of attention since they were made in the March 1989 report on "Clearance and Settlement Systems in the World's Securities Markets." The recommendations were designed to encourage the development of national standards for reducing risk and improving the efficiency of securities clearance and settlement systems worldwide. They made nine recommendations to be considered by all participating countries, including a recommendation for settlement of securities transactions within three days of the trade date.

In their November 1990 report, the United States Working Committee supported the "T+3" recommendation, stating that "moving settlement closer to the time that an actual trade is executed brings greater certainty and credibility to marketplaces . . . and will result in 'fewer trades in the pipeline' with a concomitant reduction in overall risk to the system."

The U.S. securities industry task force recommended in May 1992 that the ACH be used to comply with the T+3 recommendation for the 160 million retail security payments made annually in the United States. Under current check-based practice, settlement takes about five days. The Task Force on Clearance and Settlement Reform in U.S. Securities Markets contends that ACH payments can lower risk in two ways: there is less time for one of the parties to the transaction to default; and there is less time for the value of the securities to fluctuate if there is a default.

On the surface, ACH direct debit seems to be made to order for securities purchases, particularly for programs that call for regular consumer contributions into an investment fund. Brokers could offer an attractive consumer investment product by directly debiting the consumer's account, and at the same time, significantly shorten the duration of their own exposure to consumer defaults. The securities industry estimated that half of all retail securities payments could settle electronically within three years, so this does seem to be a major opportunity for banks who offer ACH direct debit services.

But there is a significant obstacle to overcome first. Current ACH rules—the 60-day consumer right of recision, in particular—make the risk of ACH direct debit prohibitive for securities firms and their bank service providers. Unlike check returns, Regulation E and NACHA Rules allow the consumer 60 days to notify the receiving bank of an unauthorized ACH debit or a debit made in error. Under NACHA Rules, consumers have 15 calendar days after receiving a bank statement or other form of notification of the debit to tell the receiving bank that they wish to be recredited because the debit was not authorized. The receiving bank can then send an adjustment entry to reverse the debit if the consumer's notice was sent within 60 calendar days of the original debit.

Obviously, 60 days is a completely unacceptable period of time to elapse before a broker discovers that a customer's purchase will not settle. Therefore, a rule change was proposed during 1992 that would have created a new ACH transaction type and eliminate the 60-day right of recision for securities payments. Unfortunately, NACHA rejected the proposed change.

NACHA is comprised of 40 regional automated clearing house associations who represent a wide diversity of bank members. Most large originating banks were in favor of the change, but there were enough smaller regional clearing houses representing smaller receiving banks who were opposed.

Payment of Interest and Dividends

Banks also provide securities-related stockholder services to their corporate customers. Many of the credit risks associated with check and electronic funds transfer services also apply to securities services. The risks associated with the payment of dividend, interest, and other income payments are discussed below.

Income payments have traditionally been handled with controlled disbursement and other check disbursement products. The bank's primary source of risk derives from the credit decision associated with all check disbursement products—should the bank return customer checks for insufficient funds, or should the bank take the credit risk and pay the checks? Chapter 5 discusses the many variations in risk associated with controlled disbursement funding methods. The risk assessment worksheet, risk control options, and sample risk management plan are all appropriate for securities-related disbursements.

The use of ACH for dividend disbursements is still limited, but its use is beginning to grow. Many banks have been experimenting with ACH disbursements for their own stockholders, and some are beginning to offer the service to their corporate customers. The risk issues associated with direct deposit of dividends closely parallel those discussed for direct deposit of payroll.

According to NACHA rules, the originating bank guarantees payment when it releases entries to the ACH processor—either the Federal Reserve or a private processor. This generally occurs one or two days prior to the payment date. Most banks require their corporate customers to fund their disbursement accounts by the payment date, not several days earlier when the bank releases entries to the ACH processor. The bank's account at the Federal Reserve is debited on the payment date, regardless of whether the company funded its disbursement account. The result is that the bank has in effect extended credit to its corporate customer from the time it released the credit entries to the ACH processor until it is funded by the customer on the payment date.

A company with liquidity problems could fail to fund the disbursement account or declare bankruptcy. If the bank has already released the payment entries to the ACH processor, NACHA rules preclude recalling or reversing the payment entries, even if the disbursement account is unfunded. The sequence of events that creates this credit risk was previously outlined in Figure 4-2.

Chapter 4 discusses ACH payment risk in detail. The risk assessment worksheet, risk control options, and sample risk management plan are all appropriate for securities-related disbursements.

Even though the risk management techniques in the chapters on EFT and check services apply equally to securities-based payments and more traditional cash management services, it makes sense to devise a separate risk management plan for securities services. As a practical matter, the securities area is usually a separate operating entity with distinct management goals and priorities.

7

RISK-BASED PRICING

Even though many operating services entail considerable credit risk, traditionally banks have not taken the full cost of risk management into consideration when pricing these services.

These expenses should include the cost of capital necessary to support potential losses as well as the cost of operational systems and procedures necessary to control the risk—Stage II periodic review and Stage III interactive controls.

Since few banks allocate capital to operating services on the basis of risk, the concept of risk-based pricing is foreign to most business managers of operating services. However, recent Federal Reserve policy statements that modify the measurement of daylight overdrafts and provide for the pricing of daylight overdrafts that occur in the reserve and clearing accounts of depository institutions should prompt managers to rethink their pricing strategies and add the full cost of risk management to their equations.

Federal Reserve Daylight Overdraft Pricing

The first phase of overdraft pricing—10 basis points at an annual rate for the Fedwire operating day—will go into effect on April 14, 1994. The fee will rise to 20 basis points one year later and to 25 basis points a year after that. To the extent that these fees are caused by customer overdraft positions, managers should consider the various direct and indirect ways of passing the fees on to the customer.

For the majority of banks, however, the impact of Federal Reserve daylight overdraft pricing will not be substantive since the Board estimates that fewer than 300 institutions will actually have to pay fees. Nevertheless, Federal Reserve pricing will serve to focus attention on the general issue of risk-based pricing for the entire industry.

In addition to pricing for daylight overdrafts, the Federal Reserve is considering expanding the self-assessment guide for determining the daylight overdraft cap a bank is allowed. The cap is based on a multiple of the bank's adjusted primary capital, which is determined by a number of factors, including the bank's ability to control positions across Fedwire.

A future expansion of the self-assessment guide is likely to include controls for nonwire money movements such as automated clearing house, check, and securities transactions. When this occurs, the risks associated with nonwire services will have a direct impact on a bank's daylight overdraft cap, and an indirect impact on the bank's cost of providing nonwire operating services. For instance, inclusion of ACH controls in a bank's self-assessment could result in higher costs to banks for ACH controls, especially those that allow large dollar ACH or electronic data interchange (EDI) transactions.

Payment System Concerns

General industry concerns regarding payment system issues will further focus attention on pricing. For example, some bankers are concerned that the relatively low price of automated clearing house transactions could encourage high dollar wire transfers to switch to ACH, adding risk to the overall payments system. The advent of corporate-to-corporate EDI payment formats in the mid-1980s highlights this problem, since it encourages using the ACH for high dollar payments.

Wire transfer systems are designed to handle single high dollar transactions. Security is extensive, and with same day settlement, temporal risk is slight.

On the other hand, the ACH was originally conceived as an electronic substitute for low dollar, high volume consumer checks. Future valued batch processing offers low cost delivery. ACH payments are more secure than the check payments they replaced, but they are not as secure and they create more temporal risk than wire transfers.

Federal Reserve pricing for daylight overdrafts can help prevent the unwanted migration of high dollar wire transfers to the ACH because it can increase the cost of the ACH transfer—beyond the additional cost of controls mentioned above. This happens because the Federal Reserve debits a bank's reserve account later in the day for wire transfers than for ACH credits, resulting in lower daylight overdraft fees for banks that use wire transfers for large dollar transactions. The debit to the bank's reserve account for originating ACH credits is posted at the opening of business, but debits for Fedwire transfers are posted later in the day as they actually occur.

To discourage the unwanted migration of wire transfers to the ACH, managers should consider incorporating these added costs into their pricing policies.

This example illustrates the impact that the Federal Reserve's daylight overdraft policy and other payment system concerns can have on bank pricing policies. The main impact is increased awareness of the constant need to rationalize and review pricing policies. But with or without a push from the Federal Reserve, risk-based pricing is an issue that needs more consideration as banks adopt policies to manage operating credit risk.

The next section provides an overview to the main cost considerations when reviewing the impact of risk on pricing policies for corporate services.

Risk Management Costs

There are three basic ways to manage credit risk: exposure reduction, risk control, and risk funding—and they all carry costs to consider.

Exposure Reduction

Standard banking techniques offer many creative ways to reduce risk exposure. For example, banks have traditionally adjusted their availability and collectibility schedules, within the confines of Federal Reserve Regulation CC, to reduce check collection exposure.

Similarly, banks incur credit risk when they send direct deposit of payroll credits to employee accounts through the ACH. The bank obligates itself to make the payments when it delivers the entries to its local ACH processor, usually the day before payday, even though its corporate customer is generally not required to fund the disbursement account until payday.

This credit exposure could be eliminated by requiring the customer to fund its payroll before the entries are delivered to the ACH processor. Negotiation of collateral or guarantees may also reduce credit exposure for cash management services.

Although exposure reduction techniques are generally not expensive for banks to implement, they often result in higher customer costs.

Risk Control

Programs to control risk, on the other hand, can involve changes in operations and are often expensive to implement. Stage II periodic review monitors risk after it has already occurred, but usually in enough time to alert management to take remedial action. This is a lower cost predecessor to Stage III interactive control, which is designed to monitor the actual level of risk as it changes, and to refer transactions to the proper credit authority for approval before the exposure is created. Examples of Stage III controls are the use of intraday funds control systems to manage daylight overdraft positions and the establishment of dollar limits on the size of ACH files.

Loss Funding

Provisions must also be made for any losses that do occur. Although banks insure loan losses by deducting a provision from earnings to create a reserve, most do not use this mechanism to insure against losses from operating services. Ideally, reserves should be built and capital allocated to operating services in proportion to the risks they incur.

To determine the levels of credit risk to be funded, the following have to be considered: how much risk remains after implementing exposure reduction and risk control procedures, the operational dependability of the efforts, and an analysis of the likelihood of loss from the remaining exposure.

Product and Customer Risk Components

Once the dynamics of credit risk management costs are fully understood, it is useful to analyze both product and customer specific risk components. A decision can then be made as to whether pricing should be uniform for all customers for a product, or whether customers should be categorized by risk and priced based upon the risk they contribute.

The first priority is to accurately quantify the overall costs of credit risk management for each operating service. Pricing decisions should take all costs of risk management into account.

Next, if the analysis indicates that there is a significant difference in the costs for specific customer risk grades, costs can be allocated proportionately.

A formal assessment should be conducted for each operating service if credit risk is significant. Three services are examined below in more detail for illustrative purposes: ACH credit origination, cash concentration, and controlled disbursement. Each example builds on the sample risk management plans presented in the earlier chapters on EFT, check, and securities exposures.

ACH Credit Origination

It was previously mentioned, in the context of payment system concerns, that ACH pricing could be used to discourage the unwanted migration of wire transfers to the ACH. It was also suggested that managers should take into account all of the costs associated with the added risk of ACH when formulating their pricing strategies. This section examines each of the risk management costs that should be considered, and it explores the implication of possible pricing strategies after analyzing the cost of exposure reduction, risk control, and loss funding.

The ACH credit origination risk management plan in Figure 7-1 provides a logical starting point. It was presented earlier (Figure 4-6) to illustrate the broad headings and general construct of a possible plan for managing ACH credit origination risk. This section introduces more specific assumptions to the example.

Exposure Reduction

ACH credit origination is unique in that there is a readily available method for totally eliminating all of the credit risk associated with the service. There would be no credit risk whatsoever if *all* customers were required to prefund—a practice that is usually not feasible in a competitive market.

Because of market considerations, the bank that produced the sample risk management plan in Figure 7-1 found it necessary to institute a more moderate prefunding policy. Instead of requiring all customers to prefund, only watch list customers in credit grades 6-9 are required to prefund.

Figure 7-1   ACH Credit Origination—
Risk Management Plan (with Pricing)

Sample Illustration

	Grades 6-9	Grade 5	Grades 1-4
Approval Required	No new customer approvals	Group manager Monthly review	Normal lending authority Annual review
Operation	Account administrator (Check prefunding)	Credit limits, overlimit blocks Account administrator (Check credit limits, call for credit approvals)	Standard
Credit Exposure Reduction	Prefund, or Collateral, or Guarantee	Partial collateral, or Partial guarantee	
Credit Exposure	None	Credit limit (entries released) less partial collateral or guarantee	Entries released to ACH
Operating Risk	Failure to check prefunding	Failure to check limits	

	Grades 6-9	Grade 5	Grades 1-4
Annual Revenue before Risk Pricing	$40,000	$440,000	$1,200,000
Risk Pricing	None, standard pricing (prefunding is required)	Standard	Standard
Annual Risk Revenue	$933 (annual interest on prefunding)		

The cost implication of this policy depends upon the bank's ACH system capabilities. Balance verification just prior to distribution of credit entries to the ACH processor does not guarantee that the funds will still be in the customer's disbursement account on the payment date several days later. The equivalent of a hold must be placed on the funds over the duration of the exposure. This is difficult for many banks to accomplish without exception processing. Depending on the bank, a separate dedicated account could be necessary, especially if interest is paid. It is also important to be sure that there is clear access to the funds by the bank in the event of the customer's bankruptcy.

If a bank automates the prefunding process, the ongoing operating cost is usually low once the system is in place. Most of the cost is fixed. In this example, however, the process is manual and the risk management plan indicates a need for a part-time account administrator to check for prefunding and coordinate the process. Nevertheless, we can assume that the manual administrative cost of prefunding is minimal because there are only three watch list customers.

The three customers require only 15 minutes per day by the account administrator to manually check for prefunding—or about $75 per month in allocated salary cost. Although not material in this case, the operating cost of prefunding can be significant for some banks, so it should be considered before any bank finalizes its overall pricing rationale.

The number of watch list customers on the service is not likely to grow very much beyond three in this example because no new customer approvals are allowed for credit grades 6-9. The three customers in the example were originally approved at higher grades and subsequently downgraded. Although unpopular with those customers, prefunding was accepted because they wanted to maintain the service, and they knew it would be very difficult to find another bank to offer the service without prefunding. In the final analysis, the downgraded customers realized that their loss of use of funds is not a major additional burden.

From the bank's perspective, there is an automatic offset to the administrative cost of prefunding since the bank benefits from the earlier use of the funds. If we continue to assume three prefunding customers, the added income to the bank is calculated as follows:

Income = (internal transfer rate) × (number of days prefunded/360)
         × (dollar amount of files)

For example, each of the three customers originates the following ACH files during a month:

Customer 1:   2 files of $25,000 each

Customer 2:   1 file of $50,000

Customer 3:   1 file of $10,000 and one file of $30,000

Assuming 2 days additional use of funds for each file, the bank would earn an additional $77.78 per month.

Customer 1:	$2\,[(0.1)\,(2/360)\,(25,000)]$ =	$27.78
Customer 2:	$(0.1)\,(2/360)\,(50,000)$ =	27.78
Customer 3:	$(0.1)\,(2/360)\,(10,000)$	
	$+\,(0.1)\,(2/360)\,(30,000)$ =	22.22
		$77.78

In this case, the income is not material, but it does offset the $75 administrative expense calculated earlier. Unless the administrative expense is exceptionally large at a given bank, it is not unusual to find that the cost of prefunding is offset by the additional income it creates.

In a sense, the requirement for prefunding is itself a form of risk-based pricing. The three customers in the example undoubtedly consider it part of the price—analogous to float pricing for other services. What is surprising to some bankers and customers alike is that the dollar amounts are not as large as many expect. Prefunding is not unreasonable in many situations. However, the price does increase rapidly for large dollar transactions.

For example, if a large dollar EDI related file for $3,500,000 was prefunded for one day only, the price would escalate to $972. Wire transfer is a much better alternative in this case. This example also highlights the irrationality of moving from intraday wire transfer exposure to the overnight exposures of ACH when customers are motivated by lower ACH transaction fees. Logically, high dollar ACH should be more expensive than wire transfer when risk is considered.

Another prefunding variation to consider is the possibility of paying interest on the prefunded amounts. In most cases, it is not desirable from the bank's perspective because it negates the effect of offsetting the additional administrative expense. However, in the large dollar EDI example, if wire transfer is not a viable alternative—perhaps because the necessary addenda information would be difficult to deliver without ACH addenda records—then paying interest on the prefunded amount might make sense. An alternative would be to allow the customer to use the prefunded amount as credit toward required balances for services. Again, it is not likely that a bank would encourage a new customer to enter an arrangement like this, but in the event of a downgrading of an existing customer, it is a possible alternative to discontinuing the service.

Figure 7-1 also indicates that the bank in this example considers requiring collateral or guarantees as an acceptable risk reduction measure. It is an alternative to prefunding for credit grades 6-9, and partial collateral or guarantees are required for credit grade 5 customers. For grades 6-9, collateral or guarantees might be easier to implement from an operations viewpoint than prefunding, but they do not always provide as complete protection. There is a possibility that the credit entries could exceed the collateral or guarantee. Nevertheless, collateral or guarantees provide a large measure of protection and are a serious alternative to prefunding. The economics from both the customer's and bank's point of view are similar to prefunding.

Risk Control

The second major category of risk management cost is the expense associated with risk control. The risk management plan indicates that credit grades 6-9 require no additional risk control beyond the prefunding previously discussed, grade 5 requires the establishment of interactive credit limits, above which no files will be processed without specific credit approval, and grades 1-4 require periodic review only. The assumption is that the bank has not yet installed an automated risk module for their ACH system, so the interactive control required for grade 5 customers is accomplished with manual procedures. This is feasible because of the limited number of grade 5 customers. Ideally, if the risk system is automated in the future, limits will be established for all customers.

The limited manual system for the grade 5 customers in our example is administered by one full-time person, so the added control does bring additional operating costs. If an automated system is installed in the future to enable interactive controls for all customers, the actual operating costs of processing transactions through the ACH system would probably not increase significantly. The main addition to operating cost would be the referral system to get credit approval for overlimit transactions. The referral system workload, in addition to being dependent on the total number of customers, is dependent upon how tight or loose the credit limits are in relation to the actual file sizes processed. Tight limits mean more referrals and higher operating cost, as well as possible additional problems if customer service is adversely affected. Selection of the most appropriate credit limit for each customer requires the balancing of risk, cost, and customer service considerations.

The fixed cost of installation may be the more significant cost factor if an automated system is considered. The software itself could cost in the neighborhood of $50,000, and the technical installation and internal interfaces could easily double the investment to $100,000. Regardless of whether manual or automated procedures are used, the cost of an interactive system—a system to prevent exposures before they occur—can be expensive.

Loss Funding

Finally, the costs associated with loss funding should be analyzed before finalizing a pricing strategy. Loss funding should provide protection from any credit losses that do occur after the bank has implemented its exposure reduction and risk control procedures. But, quantification of the magnitude of the remaining exposure and determining the likelihood of an actual loss can be difficult.

It is here that the blurring of various categories of risk can lead risk managers astray if they are not very careful. Even though *credit* exposure was totally eliminated in theory for credit grades 6-9 by requiring prefunding in this particular example, there is still an *operating* risk that the bank could fail to check for the need and properly execute the prefunding. Likewise, the check for credit limits, execution of overlimit blocks, and referrals for credit approval for grade 5 customers might be done improperly, especially given the manual process in our example.

The potential for *fraud* loss also distorts the problem of quantifying the remaining exposure. There is a significant fraud potential with ACH credit origination because of the delay between distribution and funding. In our example, the problem is reduced with prefunding for grade 6-9 and credit limits for grade 5 customers, but the potential for fraud can still be significant for grades 1-4.

Even though this book focuses on credit risk, loss funding should take into account all categories of risk. As a practical matter, banks will want to manage the funding of all potential sources of loss as a single issue.

The problem of quantifying the level of loss funding needed is further compounded by the fact that many times there are no actual loss histories for operating services. This is often the case for ACH credit origination, even when significant risks clearly do exist. It should also be recognized that prior history is not necessarily a valid predictor of future events.

Of the three main components of risk management—risk reduction, risk control, and loss funding—pricing for the loss funding portion will probably involve the more arbitrary cost allocations. Given the fact that the potential for loss is apparent, but the magnitude and frequency of possible future losses are difficult to quantify, how can loss funding be handled?

One answer that immediately comes to mind is to fund the risk across a broader source of exposures than ACH credit origination alone. There are at least three ways to expand the risk base to one where a loss history might be meaningful: combine ACH credit origination exposure with exposures from other operating services, combine ACH credit origination exposure with traditional lending exposure, or purchase outside insurance.

Combine with other operating services. On the surface, combining the risk of several operating services seems to be a good way to establish a meaningful pool of potential losses. If our objective, however, is to identify all of the costs of risk management that need to be included in a product pricing strategy, combining products can obscure important pricing issues.

Combining ACH credits with wire transfer provides a good example. Figure 7-2 illustrates the fundamental credit risk management costs for the two products. The impact of credit risk management on operating expense is relatively high for wire transfer, because of the intraday online process, but it is relatively low in the batch ACH environment.

If we assume that potential losses are funded using risk-based capital allocations, alternative 1 in Figure 7-2 shows that capital costs for wire transfer are relatively low compared to ACH. This occurs because intraday wire transfer exposures are not allowed by the bank, but there are overnight exposures associated with ACH.

But, there are many factors that can impact how much capital should be allocated to each product based on credit risk—a subjective judgment at best. For example, alternative 2 shows that prefunding dramatically reduces the capital required for ACH. Likewise, allowing wire transfer customers to have intraday credit limits, or higher limits, increases the capital allocation to wire transfer.

Operating risk creates yet another set of variables. Because of the high dollar amounts moved by wire transfer, errors, performance failures, and

---

Figure 7-2   Credit Risk Management Costs

	Wire Transfer	ACH Credit
Operating Controls	HIGH Intraday Online Process	LOW Batch Process
Allocated Capital Alternative 1	LOW Intraday Credit Not Allowed	HIGH Overnight Exposure
Allocated Capital Alternative 2	HIGH Intraday Credit Allowed	LOW Prefunding Required

---

external disruptions can potentially create losses far greater than those from ACH. Unlike credit loss histories, operating losses for wire transfer can be observed in historic patterns. In fact, some banks find it necessary to have dedicated compensation specialists for wire transfer, but not for ACH. Credit risk may very well take a back seat to operating and fraud risk when trying to quantify potential losses for pricing purposes.

There is little wonder that most banks do not consider risk funding in their operating credit risk management programs. Risk funding requires more than combining services into larger pools if it is to serve as a meaningful basis for a pricing strategy.

Combine with loan exposure. A more promising possibility is to combine exposures on a customer basis. In effect, this is what happens at most banks now. If a credit loss related to ACH credit origination does occur, it would undoubtedly be absorbed by the reserve for loan losses under the assumption the lending organization "owns" the relationship. Operating profits and losses from corporate services ultimately find their way through the bank's accounting system and show up on the lending unit's profit and loss statement. Pricing for risk funding becomes a relationship issue rather than a product issue.

The best way to assure that operating credit risk is properly funded is to establish a policy that requires it to be added to the total exposure reported to management for each customer. As a natural by-product, the analysis for determining the proper level for the loan loss reserve will take into account the possibility of operating credit losses. In other words, formalize the practice that currently occurs.

The loan loss reserve approach works fine for borrowing customers, but it does present problems if there are many ungraded operating customers. Probably the most prevalent example of this is found with direct deposit of payroll, a product that many banks sell through their branch systems in a nonrelationship mode. It is not unusual to find a large proportion of direct deposit customers who do not have borrowing relationships with the bank. The solution for nonborrowing customers is probably found in the risk reduction and control procedures the bank employs—in this case for direct deposit. The idea is to manage the level of risk down to where funding potential losses is not a significant problem. We saw earlier that prefunding virtually eliminates the credit risk, and the cost to the customer may not be prohibitive. If prefunding is not feasible, Stage III interactive controls are the next best way to limit exposures to predictable and manageable levels.

We assumed earlier that the lending organization has ultimate profit and loss responsibility for corporate services. But, suppose the business unit that provides the service is a profit center. Can the bank still use the loan loss reserve approach? The answer is a very qualified yes. First, after taking into account its risk reduction and risk control measures, the business unit has to decide if its remaining exposure requires funding. If it does, the business unit can consider establishing its own reserve with regular deductions from earnings, or it can negotiate a provision for operating credit losses to be applied to an existing loan loss reserve.

Regardless of the risk funding method employed—direct product pricing, combining services, or combining with loan losses—it is difficult to avoid subjective cost allocations to specific products.

Purchase insurance. The third alternative is to purchase insurance. This is probably not a feasible alternative for credit exposures, at least from the perspective of the insurance company.

But we saw earlier that fraud and operating risks are an integral part of a bank's loss funding decision. Assuming that credit risk funding is handled as a subset of the loan loss reserve, can the fraud and operating risk portions be handled with outside insurance? Some of the larger payments and cash management banks have taken this approach with success.

The main benefit of insurance from a pricing perspective is that there is a precise risk funding cost in the form of premiums payable. The cost should be part of the overall product cost structure. Fraud and operating risks apply equally across the customer base, so there is no need to allocate to specific subsets of customers.

Summary of Pricing Rationale

An approach to analyzing the need for risk-based pricing is evident. First, reduce credit exposures for ACH credit origination as much as possible, within business constraints, with prefunding and risk controls. Take the net cost of prefunding and risk controls into account when developing a pricing strategy. The costs can be allocated to customers based on credit grade, or they can be distributed across the product customer base.

Second, determine if the potential credit losses after risk reduction and risk control warrant loss funding. Many times, the remaining exposure will not warrant loss funding. If funding is required, consider a relationship approach using the loan loss reserve as the first choice. Implementation may merely require a policy of including ACH credit origination risk in a customer's total exposure. Pricing for loss funding then becomes a total relationship issue, not a product issue.

Third, with credit risk now accounted for, consider the need for loss funding for related fraud and operating risks, remembering that they may also have been reduced as a result of credit risk reduction and control. If necessary, consider purchasing insurance. There is no need to allocate insurance costs to specific subsets of customers because fraud and operating failure impacts the entire customer base equally.

The specific risk pricing, or lack of risk pricing, for the example in Figure 7-1 can be explained as follows:

- No additional pricing is required for credit grades 6-9 because prefunding is mandated by policy—virtually eliminating credit losses. The customers in that category do pay for the extra account administration time by providing the bank with earlier use of funds.

- No additional pricing is required for grade 5 customers because policy requires the risk to be partially eliminated with collateral and guarantees. Interactive controls prevent unapproved exposures from occurring. Because a limited manual process is used, the additional cost of a portion of one account administrator is not worth special pricing attention.

- The bank decided that the limited exposure that remains after the effect of its risk reduction and risk control procedures does not require specific risk funding beyond its normal reserves for credit losses.

- Related fraud and operating exposures are not insured because the bank's standard operating controls, security procedures, and backup procedures are considered adequate. They are part of the normal cost structure for ACH credit origination products.

ACH Cash Concentration

The ACH cash concentration example in Figure 7-3 provides a somewhat different set of insights into the cost dynamics of risk-based pricing. It builds on the plan presented earlier (Figure 4-12) in Chapter 4 and examines the implications of various pricing strategies after analyzing the cost of exposure reduction, risk control, and loss funding.

Exposure Reduction

The credit risk associated with ACH cash concentration arises from return item exposure. The plan in Figure 7-3 authorizes a number of ways to reduce return item exposure, including delaying availability, converting to wire transfer, and requiring collateral or guarantees. The cost to both the bank and the customer varies with the method used.

Delayed availability. Standard procedure for ACH cash concentration is to make the concentrated funds available for withdrawal on the same day the funds are credited to the concentration account. The concentration bank has a risk that concentration debits could be returned by the local banks for insufficient funds several days after the company has withdrawn the funds from the concentration account. One way to reduce this credit exposure is to delay the availability of these funds for withdrawal for several days.

Regulation CC does not apply to electronic payments, so delaying availability of funds to the customer can be an effective risk reduction technique in selected circumstances. Because the customer's prime objective is to concentrate usable funds as rapidly as possible, delayed availability is not feasible for general use in a competitive market.

Figure 7-3	**ACH Cash Concentration—**
	Risk Management Plan (with Pricing)

Sample Illustration

	Grades 6-9	Grade 5	Grades 1-4
Approval Required	No new customer approvals	Group manager Monthly review	Normal lending authority Annual review
Operation	Account administrator (Check location and file limits) Location limits, file limits	Account administrator (Check location and file limits) Location limits, file limits	Standard
Credit Exposure Reduction	Delay availability 3 days, or Require wire transfer, or Require 3 day's collateral, or Require guarantee	Partial collateral, or Partial guarantee	
Credit Exposure	None	Portion of returns	All returns
Operating Risk	Failure to check limits	Failure to check limits	

	Grades 6-9	Grade 5	Grades 1-4
Annual Revenue before Risk Pricing	$300,000	$500,000	$700,000
Risk Pricing	5% return item value	2% return item value	Standard
Annual Risk Revenue	$30,000	$25,000	

However, the sample plan does advocate the technique for the riskiest customers in watch list credit grades 6-9. Similar to ACH credit origination, the bank's policy forbids new customer approvals in watch list grades, so any watch list cash concentration customers that do exist would have been downgraded after an earlier approval at a higher grade. Downgraded customers may prefer delayed availability to termination of service.

The protection to the bank and the cost to the customer depend upon how many days are added to the availability schedule. Using the example of a retailer with 14 store locations, each concentrating $25,000 per day using ACH debits, the bank could lose over $1 million in a bankruptcy.

$$(14 \times \$25,000) \times (3 \text{ days to return}) = \$1,050,000$$

In a very serious credit crisis, the bank could delay availability three days—the estimated time required for large dollar ACH returns—and virtually eliminate its exposure.

The cost to the customer, however, would be high. Value lost at 10% interest is over $83 per day—or $1,833 per month if the arrangement continues for any length of time. The economic benefit of the product would be eliminated, so the customer's main motivation for using the service is completely negated. Nevertheless, the convenience of an automated system and the need to find an alternative during very trying times may prompt the customer to agree to the arrangement.

A compromise could be negotiated, but the bank would still risk losing $350,000 with a one day delay instead of three.

Wire transfer. A very common method for reducing return item risk is to require the customer to wire funds from the local depositories to the concentration account rather than initiate ACH debits to draw down the local accounts. This is a virtually risk free method of cash concentration for the bank.

The cost to the customer can be even higher than delayed availability—at least in this example. At $10 per wire, the cost of using wire transfer is $140 per day. Assuming that wire transfer is a profitable product, there is no additional cost from the bank's perspective.

Sometimes a compromise can be negotiated with the customer. For instance, the bank might agree to let the customer use ACH debits for low dollar locations and require wires for high dollar locations only. Even if the bank requires delayed availability for the ACH locations, the customer still benefits. The cost of delayed availability is lowest to the customer at the low dollar locations, and wire transfers are limited to a less costly number.

The point is that before the bank automatically removes a customer from the service, it should thoroughly explore all of the alternatives.

Collateral or guarantees. The possibility of requiring collateral or guarantees can also be explored. Some customers will find this option to be less onerous and less complicated to track and manage than delayed availability. The bank in our example requires at least partial collateral or guarantees for the limited number of marginal customers in credit grade 5.

With delayed availability, wire transfers, collateral, and guarantees—plus combinations of all—the bank has many options for exposure reduction. As with prefunding for ACH credits, the options are self-funding and create no additional costs that need to be considered in a pricing strategy. In fact, the customer is likely to consider each option an alternative form of risk-based pricing.

Risk Control

The second category of cost to analyze is the expense associated with risk control. There are effective ways to limit and control the exposure from cash concentration return items.

The risk management plan in Figure 7-3 indicates that customers in credit grades 5-9 also require interactive control measures as an added precaution. These credit grades require the establishment of interactive credit limits, above which no files will be processed without specific credit approval. Limits can be set on each specific location, as well as for total debit amount originated. In some cases, the data collection vendor can enforce the location limits, but the bank should have the ability to monitor and limit the overall file size.

Grades 1-4 only require periodic review in this example because the bank has not yet installed an automated risk module for their ACH system.

Interactive control is accomplished with manual procedures. This is feasible because the number of grade 5-9 customers is limited. Ideally, if the risk system is automated in the future, limits will be established for all customers.

The limited manual system is administered by the same full-time person who coordinates risk controls for ACH credit origination, so the cost of this added control is not excessive. If an automated system is installed for all customers in the future, the cost of processing transactions through the

ACH system would probably not increase significantly. The main addition to operating cost would be the referral system to get credit approval for overlimit transactions. The referral system workload, in addition to being dependent on the total number of customers, is dependent upon the magnitude of the credit limits in relation to the files processed. Tight limits mean more referrals, higher operating costs, and more customer service cost.

An automated control system for ACH would undoubtedly include both debit and credit transactions. Therefore, the same economics apply as those for credit origination. The fixed cost is significant, with software estimated at $50,000 and internal installation costs another $50,000. Regardless of whether manual or automated procedures are used, the cost of an interactive system can be high.

Loss Funding

Most of the loss funding principles discussed for ACH credit origination apply to ACH cash concentration, so they will not be repeated in detail here. The main problem is the difficulty in quantifying likely losses after considering the impact of exposure reduction and risk controls. Historic losses for specific products do not yield much insight. Blurring between credit, operating, and fraud losses complicates the problem further.

Various schemes for providing loss funding can be explored, including combining cash concentration with other services, combining cash concentration with loans on a customer relationship basis, or purchasing insurance. A workable three-step approach includes the following:

1. Apply risk reduction and risk control measures. Often, they are self-funding. If not, they can be allocated to products or customers using accepted cost accounting principles.

2. Combine cash concentration exposure with loan exposure and use the existing credit loss reserve if funding of the remaining credit risk is required.

3. Consider using insurance to fund fraud and operating risk, if necessary. The most significant risk funding problem with cash concentration may not be possible credit losses. If credit exposure is well controlled, as previously discussed, kiting and illegal practices may be the larger problem.

Summary of Pricing Rationale

The rationale for the risk pricing illustrated in Figure 7-3 is similar to the rationale for ACH credit origination pricing. For the most part, exposure reduction and risk control are self-funding, and some techniques are themselves a form of risk-based pricing. Additional risk funding to cover the cost of risk management is not needed.

However, ACH cash concentration offers a unique opportunity to employ an incentive pricing component as well. Credit exposure is created when items are returned. Unlike consumer applications where there are a large number of unrelated and diverse accounts, return items are not normally expected for cash concentration. Unless the company is in real financial difficulty, returns are usually the result of deposit reporting errors or unreported disbursements from the local accounts. They can also be symptomatic of kiting situations.

One way to discourage returns is to employ punitive pricing as a disincentive. For weaker customers, pricing can also highlight the seriousness the bank places on cash concentration returns. The sample risk management plan calls for return item pricing based on the value of any returns. Returns for customers in credit grades 6-9 are priced at 5% of the value of the returns. If a $25,000 item is returned, the customer will be charged an additional $1,200 above the normal service price—a strong incentive not to create returns. Customers in credit grade 5 would incur an additional $500 charge based on a 2% return item fee.

For illustrative purposes, the $30,000 annual risk revenue in Figure 7-3 is based upon 25 returns per year of $25,000 for all grade 6-9 customers. This example illustrates the profile of a large retail customer base in an economy where many retailers are having credit difficulties.

Controlled Disbursement

Each product has its own risk management cost dynamics, and controlled disbursement provides yet another view of the issues involved in risk-based pricing. The risk management plan in Figure 7-4 builds on the earlier plan (Figure 5-8) from Chapter 5.

Exposure Reduction

Exposure reduction techniques for controlled disbursement are more limited than those available for the two products examined earlier. The option

Figure 7-4	Controlled Disbursement Risk Management Plan (with Pricing)

Sample Illustration

	Grades 6-9	Grade 5	Grades 1-4
Approval Required	No new customer approvals.	Group manager Monthly review	Normal lending authority Annual review
Operation	Alert pocket exception processing. No ACH funding allowed.	Standard No ACH funding allowed.	Standard
Credit Exposure Reduction	Partial target balance for all customers, regardless of funding method.		Target balance for ACH funding.
Credit Exposure	Amount of daily presentment, less partial target balance.	Amount of daily presentment.	Amount of daily presentment, (less target balance, for ACH funding).
Operating Risk	Failure to return checks in timely manner.	Failure to return checks in timely manner.	Failure to return checks in timely manner.

	Grades 6-9	Grade 5	Grades 1-4
Annual Revenue before Risk Pricing	$600,000	$2,900,000	$6,600,000
Risk Pricing	10% surcharge	5% surcharge	Standard
Risk Revenue	$60,000	$145,000	

specified in the sample risk management plan is to require a target balance for at least a portion of the exposure from customers in watch list credit grades 6-9. A variation on that theme would be to require collateral or guarantees in the same amount.

A required target balance costs the bank nothing to implement because controlled disbursement works off a zero balance account. Instead of automatically setting the account to zero, the system will set the account to a positive target balance. This is another example of a self-funding exposure reduction measure because the bank earns additional revenue from the increased balance.

The increased revenue, and the cost to the customer, depends on the agreed target balance. If the customer disburses $35,000 per day, and the partial target balance is set at a little over half—or $20,000—the interest per day at a 10% annual rate would be less than six dollars. Even though the amounts are not overwhelming, they represent the economic reason for using controlled disbursement in the first place. The bank could consider allowing the target balance to be applied to required balances for the service.

An important aspect of controlled disbursement is that credit exposure to a very large degree depends on the funding method used. Next day ACH funding carries more risk than same day book or wire transfers, and ACH debit funding is even more risky. Therefore, only customers in credit grades 1-4 are allowed ACH funding in the sample risk management plan.

Risk Control

The bank's controlled disbursement risk control options are even more limited than its risk reduction options. Chapter 5 discussed the fact that the main credit exposure associated with controlled disbursement does not arise from the timing and mechanics of the check clearing system or the bank's product operation. Rather, the bank's conscious decision not to return checks for insufficient funds is the main source of credit risk. Chapter 5 then discussed various ways of reducing the account officers' information gap so there is more time to make a reasoned return decision. The measures discussed were to be applied to all customers equally as standard operating procedure, not applied as special risk precautions for a subset of customers.

The one exception was to consider the use of a separate pocket during check processing to out-sort the checks of watch list customers. This would facilitate the return process if a decision was made to return checks. The sample risk management plan calls for alert pocket processing for the weakest credit risks. The incremental expense for the bank is slight since the number of customers on alert processing is very small.

Loss Funding

Exposure reduction and risk control measures for controlled disbursement help, but they do not directly attack the main source of credit exposure—the decision not to return checks. This tends to put more reliance on risk funding as a risk management technique.

The check return decision can create a classic banking exposure that is typical of all check disbursement accounts, regardless of whether controlled disbursement is used. A strong argument can be made that the possibility of credit losses from unfunded check disbursements should be included when evaluating the sufficiency of the reserve for credit losses. As mentioned above for ACH credit origination and cash concentration, in all likelihood, this operating credit risk is already funded by the reserve for credit losses on a less formal basis because any losses that do occur are absorbed by the lending unit responsible for the relationship, unless corporate services are run under a separate profit center.

Summary of Pricing Rationale

Several additional factors have been introduced by the controlled disbursement example: the specific cost components of risk management are even more difficult to quantify than in the prior examples. This compounds the difficulty in allocating risk management cost to specific subsets of customers unless one makes the general assumption that customers in riskier credit grades are more likely to cause losses for the bank than those with less credit risk.

The risk-based pricing indicated in Figure 7-4 is not based on precise allocations. Instead, the plan calls for a flat surcharge of 10% for customers in grades 6-9, 5% for customers in grade 5, and standard pricing for the rest. It is a pragmatic approach that attempts to introduce an element of fairness into the pricing strategy. If the overall product cost structure includes a provision deducted from earnings to fund possible losses, why should all customers share the cost equally if the bank decides to pass it on? The likelihood of the bank suffering a loss by not returning checks is much greater for watch list customers than the most creditworthy customers. This approach is not dissimilar to the accepted practice of charging interest on loans based on a spread from a prime rate or reference rate. Riskier customers are priced at a higher rate.

In the interests of simplicity, the surcharge is applied to normal volume-based pricing. The required information is already available for the bank's standard per check charges. A more specifically risk-based approach would be to charge a graduated percentage of the dollar amounts of the checks cleared, but this information may be more difficult to obtain for an operational "billing" process.

Product Profitability

The same surcharge concept can be used for a portfolio of products to enhance product profitability. For illustrative purposes, Figure 7-5 combines the three services previously analyzed and illustrates the potential impact of a risk surcharge on total product revenue. Total revenue generated by the three-product portfolio can be increased in the range of $47,000 to $572,000, depending upon the size of the surcharge. The middle scenario generates $286,000 in additional revenue, or a little over 2% of total annual revenue.

A 2% revenue increase can have a significant impact on product profitability. Assume the portfolio has a 30% profit margin and earns $3,984,000 net pretax on $13,280,000 total annual revenue. The additional $286,000 risk surcharge increases the net pretax to $4,270,000, or a 7% increase in net pretax earnings.

There are many variations on this theme. For instance, instead of increasing total revenue, scenarios can be analyzed where prices are lowered for less risky customers and prices are increased for the riskier ones.

Market Acceptance

Not all of the ideas discussed in this chapter will be accepted in the marketplace, but they are more likely to be accepted than they were several years ago. With regulatory pressures on banks to increase their vigilance over operating credit risk, and with the Federal Reserve instituting risk-based pricing in the form of daylight overdraft charges, the topic is being discussed.

Riskier customers require increased monitoring and controls and higher capital allocation. For perceived value, most customers are willing to pay a reasonable margin over legitimate costs. Just as in lending, those customers that represent the greater credit risk to the bank should be willing to pay a premium to cover additional costs. The growing acceptance by weaker companies that they be required to prefund ACH disbursement accounts is an example of a beginning trend. Another example is the importance of risk issues when banks and corporations negotiate pricing for EDI services.

Although it is happening very slowly, banks and their corporate customers are becoming more sophisticated in dealing with risk.

8

SUMMARY OF THE RISK
MANAGEMENT PROCESS

Techniques for managing operating credit risk build on the broad principles
of risk management that are already deeply ingrained in banking practice.
This book applies the risk management discipline already in wide use to
credit risks associated with electronic funds transfer, check, and securities
services. These "non-credit" corporate services often carry considerable
credit risk, to the point where active participation by the credit administration department with senior management review and approval is necessary.

A basic model for risk management was published by the American
Bankers Association in 1984. *Risk Assessments: The Risk Management Process*,
by H. Felix Kloman and Douglas G. Hoffman, provides a concise overview
of the process. They summarize risk management as a circle (Figure 8-1) of
interrelated and continuing steps: exposure identification, risk assessment,
risk control, and risk finance.

Exposure identification is a continuous discovery process where alternative scenarios are explored as the operating environment changes over
time. The operating environment includes external legal, regulatory and
payments system factors, customer behavior patterns, and internal bank
policies, procedures and product features. Exposure identification is an

---

**Figure 8-1   Administering the Risk Management Process—
                   A Systematic and Continuing Effort**

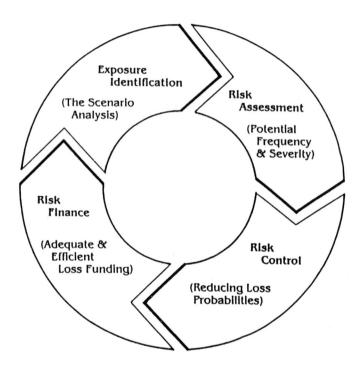

Source: American Bankers Association

---

ongoing "what- if" analysis to understand the dynamics of exposure creation.

Risk assessment attempts to measure the potential frequency and severity of the exposures that have been identified. In the context of operating credit risk, it includes the continuous measurement of past and projected dollar flows associated with customers and products and the continuous evaluation of customer creditworthiness. The process is supported with regular reports to alert management of any changes in risk assessment.

Risk control is the application of techniques to reduce the probability of loss, ranging from informal control, to periodic review, to interactive control. The key component of cost-effective risk control is the business decision that balances the trade-off between the cost of increased risk control with a reduced potential for financial loss.

Risk finance is the provision of sufficient funds to meet loss situations as they occur. Funding can be accomplished by using a variety of internal and external financial resources, including insurance and risk-based pricing.

The glue that holds this circle of continuing steps together is risk management administration. Effective administration requires a clear policy by the board of directors, senior management commitment, designated responsibility for the function, commitment by operating officers, and periodic reports to the board.

The Office of the Comptroller of the Currency and the Federal Reserve Board are reinforcing the need for effective administration of the operating credit risk management process. The OCC's Banking Circular 235 requires written policies for the assessment and ongoing monitoring of payments system risk, with top management approval, and it requires audit to be included in the review and compliance with these policies. The Federal Reserve Board's self-assessment guide is being updated to require each institution's board of directors to approve risk controls for a broader range of payments system exposures than previously required.

Getting Started

Administering a process to manage operating credit risk demands a unique blend of expertise. An effective administrator requires a working knowledge of credit administration, product operations, and product marketing. If one individual does not have the requisite knowledge, then the process must ensure that the needed lines of communication are established between the areas of the bank with the needed expertise. This requires cooperation—unprecedented in many banks—between credit administration, the non-credit business units which provide corporate services, and the corresponding operating areas.

This book provides valuable guidance in setting up the risk management process. The prior chapters furnish the necessary tools. This chapter organizes the tools in a way that enables a bank to perform the initial exposure identification and risk assessment, make decisions on what risk controls are necessary, and examine the need for risk-based pricing. Once the process is initiated, it will continue to evolve in response to specific business needs at each bank.

Five-Step Approach

The five-step approach outlined in Figure 8-2 and described below can be used to perform an initial risk management study. The objective of the study should be twofold.

1. The primary objective should be to demonstrate to senior management whether there is a business necessity to administer a formal risk management process.

2. The study should also integrate policy, procedure, and documentation in a way that demonstrates the outline of an effective ongoing process. Each interlinking element of the process should be a clear and useful prerequisite to the others.

Step 1: Analyze Customer Base

The first step is to analyze the overall creditworthiness of the customer base for each corporate service. Experience shows that a simple report indicating the names of the customers in watch list credit grades is the best way to focus senior management attention on the problem of operating credit risk. Invariably, there is at least one, and often several, well-known poor credit risks that show up on the list for a high credit risk product. The inevitable management question is: Why are we doing this?

A report format similar to Figure 4-3 is an effective way to illustrate specific exposures and generate the needed management interest. The initial analysis can be somewhat simpler than Figure 4-3 because it need not include more than one month's data to dimension the problem, and the existing exposure can be documented more concisely by only detailing the names of watch list customers for the initial presentation. Graphs like the one in Figure 2-2 can be used to provide an overall picture of the creditworthiness of each product's customer base and the relative magnitude of the exposures. They also provide an overview of the number of ungraded customers with unknown credit quality.

Figure 8-2   **Initiating the Risk Management Process**

Step 1: Analyze Customer Base

--Product Watch Lists
--Credit Grade Distributions
--Ungraded Customers

Step 2: Prepare Product Risk Profiles

--Service Description
--Credit Risk Description
--Customer Risk Calculation
--Action Steps for Deteriorating Credits

Step 3: Recommend Approval and Review Procedures

--Policy Changes
--Thresholds for Action
--Supporting Reports and Forms
--Implementation Steps and Priorities

Step 4: Recommend Product Improvements (Optional)

--Product Features
--Control Procedures
--Customer Agreements

Step 5: Recommend Pricing Strategy (Optional)

--Product Rationale
--Risk Funding

Step 2: Prepare Product Risk Profiles

Product risk profiles can be used during the initial presentation to senior management as reference materials to describe how operating credit risk arises. Equally important, if properly designed, they should become an integral part of any subsequent ongoing risk management process.

Excessive length is counterproductive, so each product profile should be brief and to the point. One product can be clearly presented in about three pages under the following headings: service description, credit risk description, customer risk calculation, and action steps for deteriorating credit.

1. Service description—an overview of the service as it is described in the bank's marketing materials.

2. Credit risk description—a more detailed section that describes how credit exposure arises. It explains the timing and mechanics of the credit exposure, legal or regulatory impacts, and current market practices.

3. Customer risk calculation—the precise formulas that should be used to calculate the exposure any given customer generates.

4. Action steps for deteriorating credit—a description of the options available if a corporate customer is downgraded or files for bankruptcy. Some institutions also include escalation instructions, with names and telephone numbers, for a customer credit crisis.

The profiles are streamlined versions of the information that was presented in Chapters 4 through 6 describing the credit risks associated with EFT, check, and securities services.

It is important that each one of the product risk profiles stand on its own as a self-explanatory document. A modular design allows the profiles to be used individually, perhaps to be inserted in a relevant customer credit file, or to be used together in a reference booklet. They should be designed for multiple use, including to do the following:

- Serve as a general fact base for corporate risk policy.
- Facilitate effective communication between the business unit, credit policy officers, and operations area regarding risk issues.
- Facilitate comparison of risk levels between products as risk dynamics change.
- Help determine when changes to the control process are necessary.
- Be useful as a training tool for product specialists and relationship officers.
- Facilitate internal audit reviews to ensure compliance with policy and procedure.

- Provide documentation for regulatory compliance, including the Office of the Comptroller of the Currency's Banking Circular 235.

Step 1 and Step 2 together accomplish the exposure identification portion of the generic risk management process in Figure 8-1. The next segment of the circle, risk assessment, can be facilitated by using the product risk assessment worksheets presented in earlier chapters. If management then decides that an ongoing risk assessment process is needed, it can be supported by up-to-date product profiles and regular management reports of customer creditworthiness and product usage.

The risk assessment process will enable management to set and adjust priorities for risk control, which leads to the next step for an initial risk management study—recommendations dealing with approval and review procedures.

Step 3: Recommend Approval and Review Procedures

First, recommendations should describe overall policies to guide new customer approvals and the periodic review of existing customers, similar to the way they were presented in Chapter 2. The main focus is on decision thresholds (credit grade, product type, dollar exposure) that trigger a given action. For instance, in Figure 2-4, customers with credit grades 1-4 require annual review, but customer credit grades 5-9 trigger a requirement for monthly tracking of each customer's exposure.

Threshold recommendations should be based on a thorough analysis of the data collected and the priorities established after Steps 1 and 2. They should balance the trade-offs between the concerns dictated by prudent risk management and the need to meet strategic revenue goals. Approval and review thresholds should not be so loose that they are ineffective and allow potentially dangerous exposures, or so tight that they become an obstacle to appropriate sales efforts.

Once overall policies are established, specific procedures can be recommended in the form of risk management plans for each individual product with credit risk (see Figure 4-6, for example) and a specifically designed approval form (see Figure 2-3).

Each risk management plan should include the approval and review procedures, required controls, and risk reduction measures required at each threshold, as well as action steps for customers with deteriorating credit quality. The controls that are specified should incorporate periodic review and interactive control techniques as appropriate.

Execution of these recommendations and plans comprises the risk control portion of the continuous risk management circle, along with Step 4 below if necessary.

Step 4: Recommend Product Improvements (Optional)

Recommendations for product improvements are not mandatory for the initial risk management study, although they are often a natural extension of product risk management plans. The need for product level risk control recommendations depends on the seriousness of any existing weaknesses.

The purpose of the initial study—to demonstrate the business rationale for risk management and initiate an evolving process—can usually be served by concentrating on improving the approval and review process first. The approval and review process assures that well-informed business decisions are made regarding risk.

In some cases, if the only reasonable decision is to not approve exposures related to certain products, restructuring of the product should be part of the initial study. Usually other factors besides credit risk come into play. The most common example is the security associated with ACH products, particularly in light of Article 4A of the Uniform Commercial Code. Article 4A requires more stringent security procedures than many banks currently provide for ACH products.

Article 4A applies to all credit transfers, including those over CHIPS, Fedwire, and the ACH, except consumer transactions covered by the Electronic Funds Transfer Act (EFTA). Check and ACH debit transactions are not covered by Article 4A.

Conformance to 4A may be a more pressing problem than credit risk to the bank, but it might also be opportune to package security and credit concerns together when designing new procedures and negotiating with customers. Besides specific product features and control procedures, recommendations may include suggested changes to customer legal agreements.

EDI (electronic data interchange) provides a second example of when it might make sense to recommend product improvements during an initial risk management study. Large dollar transactions can create risks that warrant interactive controls that were previously unnecessary for small dollar ACH applications.

Step 5: Recommend Pricing Strategy (Optional)

Pricing strategy is not a critical component of most initial risk management studies, although it is important to articulate a basic risk funding approach for the long run, even if risk-based pricing is not used.

There are circumstances, however, when pricing needs to be addressed early in the process. One example is in situations where ACH is being used by customers to replace higher priced wire transfers. Growing demand for ACH-based EDI services provides another example. Management may think that conventional ACH pricing is inappropriate when the level of credit risk is considered.

APPENDIX A

VII. EXAMINATION PROCEDURES

Operational Controls, Policies, and Procedures

B. Monitoring Customer Positions

	YES	NO
1. Has the institution identified customers who regularly participate in a large volume of wire transfer activity or in frequent large wire transfers?	___	___
2. Are criteria for placement of names on the list reasonable?	___	___
3. Can the institution monitor these accounts, taking into account the source of significant transactions?	___	___
4. Do the monitoring systems include the opening collected balance?	___	___
5. Is there a system in place to update the customer's balance reflecting intraday activity? Is the frequency appropriate?	___	___

	YES	NO

6. Does the overall system for monitoring positions of customers cover:

    a. All significant sources generating customer account entries? ___ ___

    b. Total transactions over established dollar limits? ___ ___

    c. Overdraft limits? ___ ___

    d. Single transfer limits? ___ ___

7. Are daily transactions reports generated and reviewed? ___ ___

8. Have transaction limit guidelines been established?

    a. If yes, are guidelines reasonable? ___ ___

    b. Do transaction limits include a $50 million par value size limit on secondary market book-entry Fedwire transfers? ___ ___

    c. Are guidelines reviewed regularly? ___ ___

9. Does the system halt any transaction in excess of the established limits until appropriate action is taken? ___ ___

10. If documentation of action taken with regard to over limit transactions reflects consistent exceptions attributed to a customer, is analysis of those accounts intensified? ___ ___

11. Is staff trained in exception procedures? ___ ___

12. Are exception reports generated and reviewed? ___ ___

13. Do exception reports reflect all activity in excess of transaction limits? ___ ___

	YES	NO

14. Do internal or external auditors review the funds transfer environment at least annually? (These reviews should conform to the standards established by the Bank Administration Institute and the Federal Financial Institutions Examinations Council.)   ___   ___

15. Are auditors independent?   ___   ___

16. Do audit reports reflect weaknesses in physical controls?   ___   ___

17. Are audit exception clearing procedures adequate?   ___   ___

18. Does the institution frequently incur daylight overdrafts and send large funds transfers to affiliated banks?   ___   ___

   a. Are controls in place to ensure that these extensions of credit stay within approved lines?   ___   ___

   b. Have limits been adhered to?   ___   ___

   c. Have over limit extensions been approved at the appropriate level of management?   ___   ___

19. Are transfers to affiliates   ___   ___

   a. Made pursuant to written agreement?   ___   ___

   b. Approved by the board of directors?   ___   ___

Rating

The institution should be rated according to the following guide:

____ Strong   Responses to all of the above are positive, and comprehensive customer monitoring is in force for both debits and credits on a real time basis or at least intervals of 15 minutes or less.

___ Satisfactory   Responses to all of the above are positive, and comprehensive customer monitoring is in force for all debit transactions greater than or equal to the monitoring threshold on a real time basis or at intervals of 30 minutes or less.

___ Unsatisfactory   Any other condition

a. Provide a brief discussion of the institution's monitoring system, specifically analyzing consistency between monitoring procedures in use and volume of the institution's wire transfer activity.

b. Is the institution's self-assessment consistent with guidelines?

c. If the institution's self-assessment rating is not consistent with guidelines, has management developed sufficient data to support the inconsistency?

d. If the inconsistency is not adequately supported, does management plan to reassess the rating?

APPENDIX B

OFFICE OF THE COMPTROLLER OF THE CURRENCY

BANKING CIRCULAR 235

MAY 10, 1989

To: Chief Executive Officers of All National Banks,
Deputy Comptrollers, District Administrators,
and All Examining Personnel

Purpose:

To alert national banks to the risks associated with large dollar payments systems, particularly within the international sector. Management is expected to adopt sound policies and supervisory practices for these activities. This Office recognizes that these risks are more prevalent in larger banks. However, all national banks participating in payments systems, domestic and international, must assess these risks.

Issue:

The worldwide exchange of financial transactions and information is expanding rapidly. An interlocking network of national and international markets, operating 24 hours a day, supports this activity. This network involves multiple payments, clearing, and settlement systems that handle trillions of dollars daily. In recent years, attention by bankers and regulators has focused on the operational, liquidity, and credit risks of large dollar payments systems. However, this attention mainly addressed national systems such as FEDWIRE and the Clearing House for Interbank Payments

(CHIPS). International payments, clearing, and settlement systems also demand a high level of supervision and risk assessment.

Key to each system is the *credit quality* of its participants and its *operational reliability*. These vary widely among systems and countries. A weakness in either or both of these attributes can disrupt the system and possibly cause it to fail. This may occur if a creditor in a given system cannot settle, if the support systems cannot operate, or if there is sovereign intervention. A failure in one system could pose a liquidity problem for participants in that system. If the liquidity risk is not contained, for example, through government guarantees or some participant allocation, the crisis can become systemic. The crisis can spread rapidly from participating banks to nonparticipants because of the interlocks between systems and banks.

The underlying risks remain the same for both national and international systems. However, the limited ability to influence policies and controls in international markets increases the degree of risk to national banks.

Policy:

Management of each national bank is responsible for assessing risk in each payments, clearing, and settlement system in which the bank participates. Management must adopt adequate policies, procedures, and controls with respect to these activities. At a minimum, written policies should:

- Require periodic risk assessment of each system in which the bank participates;
- Identify responsibility for assessing risks;
- Document procedures to perform the assessments;
- Require top management approval of participation in selected systems;
- Establish a process to monitor ongoing payments systems risks;
- Require written agreements between the bank and both its customers and the network; and
- Include audit in the review and compliance with these policies.

Additional detail on the risks in settlement systems is included in the Appendix to this circular.

Originating Office: Bank Information Systems Policy Division
(202) 447-4068

Robert J. Herrmann, Senior Deputy Comptroller
for Bank Supervision - Policy

INTERNATIONAL PAYMENTS SYSTEMS RISK
APPENDIX

The risks in payment systems may be divided into three broad categories:

- credit (or counterparty) risks,
- sovereign risks, and
- operational risks.

The control process to assess risk and monitor ongoing activities must consider payment systems as a whole. Although individual risks exist, they are interrelated. The effect of a single event creates additional risks within the system. For example, the effect of a single participant failing to meet its credit obligation may cause the *system* not to settle. As such, credit and settlement risk are interrelated. In another example, an operational breakdown in the system or sovereign action disrupts payments flow. The system, in turn, does not settle and credit obligations are not met. This example involves operations, settlement, and credit risk within the system.

Senior management must be both aware of and able to monitor exposure. Operating units of some banks are located throughout the world and may be participating in a number of payments systems. To control risk in these situations, some degree of centralized review is needed. This is particularly important in banks where local business units have significant autonomy. These banks may rely on local management to assess and manage the risks of participating in a payments system. However, the success or failure of one system may affect others in the network. Therefore, a bank's interdependency between systems also must be considered.

The control banks can exert over the systems in which they participate often is limited. A bank normally does not own or operate the systems. Bank management therefore must establish a process that assists them in:

- Understanding the risks posed by participation in payment systems;
- Identifying bank policies designed to manage these risks; and
- Implementing procedures and operational controls to manage risk.

The following briefly identifies several control issues, types of settlement systems, and associated risks. These are not all encompassing. Much more detail is needed to perform a comprehensive risk assessment on any settlement system.

Other references include two recently published reports on this issue.

1) Report on Netting Schemes—February 1989—prepared by the Group of Experts on Payment Systems of the central banks of the Group of Ten Countries

2) Clearance and Settlement Systems in the World's Securities Markets— March 1989—prepared by the Group of Thirty

CONTROL ISSUES

Management needs to consider and resolve numerous issues when participating in payment systems. These issues are generally the same for both national and international systems.

Guidelines should consider:

- Controls to reduce sender and receiver risks. These should include:
  — Bilateral credit limits.
  — Debit cap limits, including the process to determine these limits.
  — A process to monitor and control these limits on a real time basis.

- Controls to limit the overall exposure of the system, including debit cap limits.

- Requirements of the system to ensure that settlement occurs. This should address:
  — Conditions for settlement such as the location, time, and settling procedures.
  — The type of settlement (i.e., provisionality or finality of payment).
  — The guarantor(s), if any, of payment finality. This may involve a central bank, the system owner/operator, and/or the system participants.
  — The basis for providing necessary liquidity to the system. This may require allocation of funding by participants, coinsurance, or central bank guarantees.

- Legal issues governing the system operation, including local laws, business practices, and government regulation.

- The capabilities of the system and the bank to handle emergency situations. This may require backup operations or the ability for the bank to bypass the network.

- Responsibility for reviewing the bank's participation in payment systems.

SETTLEMENT SYSTEMS

NET SETTLEMENT SYSTEMS

Net settlement systems are systems in which transactions accumulate during a processing day. Transactions are posted to participant accounts on a provisional basis until final settlement. At end of the day, net debit positions pay, net credit positions settle, and all transactions become final. CHIPS is this type of system.

MATCHED SETTLEMENT SYSTEMS

Matched settlement systems are systems in which each transaction is "matched" by comparing messages from both counterparties to the transaction. Only exactly matched messages are allowed to enter the system to form a transaction. At the end of the processing day, the matched transactions become the basis for payment instructions issued to participants' clearing banks. Once payment is made, a transaction becomes final. CEDEL is this type of system.

GUARANTEED SETTLEMENT SYSTEMS

Guaranteed settlement systems are systems in which payment finality is guaranteed by a central bank. Because payments are irrevocable, they eliminate risk to the receiver of funds. There is no credit risk to participants in such a system. However, the sovereign and operational risks may remain. A good example of this type of system is FEDWIRE, in which the Federal Reserve guarantees payment and finality. That system is still subject to potential risks from government action or operational failure.

SYSTEM RISKS

CREDIT RISKS

Sender risk. Sender risk is the risk that a depository assumes when it makes an irrevocable payment on behalf of the customer through an extension of credit. Credit can be extended explicitly, by granting a loan, or implicitly, by paying against uncollected or provisional funds or against insufficient balances.

Receiver risk. Receiver risk involves risk to an institution upon acceptance of funds from the sender. This may be a customer, another institution, or the payments system. As the receiver of funds, an institution must rely on the sender's ability to settle its obligations at the end of the day. Receiver risk is present when payments are revocable within the system until final settlement.

SETTLEMENT RISKS

Settlement risk is the risk that each participant in the system will be able to honor all obligations at time of settlement. If one participant fails to settle, this may disrupt settlement for other participants. As a result, the system's settlement fails. This also is referred to as liquidity risk. Like receiver risk, settlement risk is present when payments are conditional or revocable until final settlement. Settlement risk also is an exposure subject to operational disruptions or sovereign actions.

NET SETTLEMENT RISKS

Net settlement risks bear all the risk identified above. However, an additional risk is that of default by the system itself. The system serves as a clearing mechanism for all transactions. At settlement, it posts a net debit or credit position to each participant's account. Each participant in a net debit position must provide funds to settle its position. If unable to settle, the *system* must cover the shortfall. If not, netted transactions unwind and other participants are affected.

The financial strength of the net settlement system itself, therefore, is a significant factor to assess. Often, this is provided through member pro rata guarantees or allocations. Also, the system's membership standards and operating procedures should ensure that the creditworthiness or operating practices of its members do not endanger the functioning of the system.

MATCHED SETTLEMENT SYSTEM RISKS

Credit risk in a matched settlement system should be addressed in the same way as for any bank customer. In matched systems the counterparty may be monitored and controlled through establishment of credit limits.

However, even in matched settlement systems attention should be given to the system's membership standards and operating procedures. The default of a participant may still impact a bank which has no settlements outstanding with it by the effect of the default on other participants with whom a bank does have outstanding settlements.

SYSTEMIC RISKS

Systemic risk is an outgrowth of settlement risk. The failure of one participant to settle deprives other institutions of expected funds and prevents those institutions from settling in turn. To the extent that chains of obligations develop, it is possible for a participant doing no business at all with a failed institution to suffer because of the effect of the failed institution on an intermediate participant and its ability to settle.

LEGAL RISKS

Any transaction occurring in a payments system is subject to the interpretation of courts in different countries and legal systems. This issue is normally addressed by the adoption of "governing law" provisions in the rules of the systems themselves. These provide for all disputes between members to be settled under the laws of a specific jurisdiction. However, they may be of limited value if a local court refuses to recognize the jurisdiction of a foreign court. This is difficult to address because there is no binding system of international commercial law for electronic payments. Banks should seek legal opinions regarding the enforceability of transactions settled through a particular system.

SOVEREIGN RISKS

Sovereign risk applies to all types of payments systems. It is the risk that action by a government may affect either a system or particular participants in a system. This action could be detrimental to other participants in the system. An example of this risk would be the imposition of exchange control regulations on a bank participating in international foreign exchange activities. While the bank itself may be both willing and able to settle its positions, government intervention prevents it from doing so. This risk can be controlled by monitoring a bank's exposure to counterparties located in nations where this type of action is considered possible.

OPERATIONAL RISKS

Operational risks include:

a) system failure - caused by a breakdown in the hardware and/or software supporting the system. This may result from design defects, insufficient system capacity to handle transaction volumes, or mechanical breakdown, including tele-communications.

b) system disruption - the system is unavailable to process transactions. This may be caused by system failure, destruction of the facility (natural disasters, fires, terrorism), or operation shutdown (employee actions, business failure, or government action).

c) system compromise - resulting from fraud, malicious damage to data, or error.

The loss of availability of the payment system from whatever source can adversely affect major participants, their correspondents, markets, and interdependent networks.

Operational risks should be controlled by the banks through a sound system of internal controls including physical security, data security, systems testing, segregation of duties, backup systems, and contingency planning. In addition, a comprehensive audit program to assess risks, adequacy of controls, and compliance with bank policies is essential.

Since most banks are third party participants in international networks, their ability to influence controls is limited. Nevertheless, they must recognize risks to their own business operations and compensate through their own internal controls. In addition, banks should exercise their influence over third party systems to the extent possible to insist upon sound operations for system continuity and integrity.

APPENDIX C

REGULATION CC

AVAILABILITY OF FUNDS AND COLLECTION OF CHECKS

12 CFR 229; Effective September 1, 1988

EXCERPTS

SECTION 229.12—Permanent Availability Schedule

(a) *Effective date.* The permanent availability schedule contained in this section is effective September 1, 1990.

(b) *Local checks and certain other checks.* A depositary bank shall make funds available for withdrawal not later than the second business day following the banking day on which funds are deposited, in the case of—

    (1) A local check;

    (2) A check drawn on the Treasury of the United States that is not governed by the availability requirements of section 229.10(c);

    (3) A check drawn on the treasury of the United States that is deposited at a nonproprietary ATM;

    (4) A U.S. Postal Service money order that is not governed by the availability requirements of section 229.10(c); and

(5)   A check drawn on a Federal Reserve Bank or a Federal Home Loan Bank; a check drawn by a state or unit of general local government; or a cashier's check, certified, or teller's check, if any check referred to in this paragraph (b)(5) is a local check that is not governed by the availability requirements of section 229.10(c).

(c)   *Nonlocal checks*

(1)   *In general.* A depository bank shall make funds deposited in an account by a check available for withdrawal not later than the fifth business day following the banking day on which funds are deposited, in the case of—

(i)   A nonlocal check; and

(ii)   A check drawn on a Federal Reserve Bank or a Federal Home Loan Bank; a check drawn by a state or unit of general local government; a cashier's, certified, or teller's check; or a check deposited in a branch of the depository bank and drawn on the same or another branch of the same bank, if any check referred to in this paragraph (c)(1)(ii) is a nonlocal check that is not governed by availability requirements of section 229.10(c).

(2)   Nonlocal checks specified in appendix B-2 to this part must be made available for withdrawal not later than the times prescribed in that appendix.

(d)   *Time period adjustment for withdrawal by cash or similar means.* A depositary bank may extend by one business day the time that funds deposited in an account by one or more checks subject to paragraphs (b) or (c) of this section are available for withdrawal by cash or similar means. Similar means include electronic payment, issuance of a cashier's or teller's check, or certification of a check, or other irrevocable commitment to pay, but do not include the granting of credit to a bank, a Federal Reserve Bank, or a Federal Home Loan Bank that presents a check to the depository bank for payment. A depository bank shall, however, make $400 of these funds available for withdrawal by cash or similar means not later than 5:00 p.m. on the business day on which the funds are available under paragraphs (b) and (c) of this section. This $400 is in addition to the $100 available under section 229.10 (c)(1)(vii).

(e) *Extension of schedule for certain deposits in Alaska, Hawaii, Puerto Rico, and the U.S. Virgin Islands.* The depositary bank may extend the time periods set forth in this section by one business day in the case of any deposit, other than a deposit described in section 229.10, that is—

   (1) Deposited in an account at a branch of a depositary bank if the branch is located in Alaska, Hawaii, Puerto Rico, or the U.S. Virgin Islands; and

   (2) Deposited by a check drawn on or payable at or through a paying bank not located in the same state as the depositary bank.

SECTION 229.13—Exceptions

(a) *New Accounts*

   (1) A deposit in a new account—

      (i) Is subject to the requirements of section 229.10(a) and (b) to make funds from deposits by cash and electronic payments available for withdrawal on the business day following the banking day of deposit or receipt;

      (ii) Is subject to the requirements of section 229.10(c)(1)(i) through (v) and section 229.10(c)(2) only with respect to the first $5,000 of funds deposited on any one banking day; but the amount of the deposit in excess of $5,000 shall be available for withdrawal not later than the ninth business day following the banking day on which funds are deposited; and

      (iii) Is not subject to the availability requirements of sections 229.10(c)(1)(vi) and (vii), 229.11, and 229,12.

      For purposes of this paragraph, checks subject to section 229.10(c)(1)(v) include traveler's checks.

(2)   An account is considered a new account during the first 30 calendar days after the account is established. An account is not considered a new account if each customer on the account has had, within 30 calendar days before the account is established, another account at the depositary bank for at least 30 calendar days.

(b)   *Large deposits.* Sections 229.11 and 229.12 do not apply to the aggregate amount of deposits by one or more checks to the extent that the aggregate amount is in excess of $5,000 on any one banking day. For customers that have multiple accounts at a depositary bank, the bank may apply this exception to the aggregate deposits to all the customer accounts held by the customer, even if the customer is not the sole holder of the accounts and not all of the holders of the accounts are the same.

(c)   *Redeposited checks.* Section 229.11 and 229.12 do not apply to a check that has been returned unpaid and redeposited by the customer or the depository bank. This exception does not apply—

(1)   To a check that has been returned due to a missing indorsement and redeposited after the missing indorsement has been obtained, if the reason for return indication on the check states that it was returned due to a missing indorsement; or

(2)   To a check that has been returned because it was postdated, if the reason for return indicated on the check states that it was returned because it was postdated, and if the check is no longer postdated when redeposited.

(d)   *Repeated overdrafts.* If any account or combination of accounts of a depositary bank's customer has been repeatedly overdrawn, then for a period of six months after the last such overdraft, sections 229.11 and 229.12 do not apply to any of the accounts. A depositary bank may consider a customer's account to be repeatedly overdrawn if—

(1)   On six or more banking days within the preceding six months, the account balance is negative, or the account balance would have become negative if checks or other charges to the account had been paid; or

(2)   On two or more banking days within the preceding six months, the account balance is negative, or the account balance would have been negative, in the amount of $5,000 or more, if checks or other charges to the account had been paid.

(e)   *Reasonable cause to doubt collectibility.*

(1)   *In general.* If a depositary bank has reasonable cause to believe that the check is uncollectible from the paying bank, then section 229.10(c)(1)(iii) and (v); section 229.10(c)(2) to the extent that it applies to a check drawn on a Federal Reserve Bank or a Federal Home Loan Bank, or a cashier's or teller's, or certified check; section 229.11; and section 229.12 do not apply with respect to a check deposited in an account at a depositary bank. Reasonable cause to believe a check is uncollectible requires the existence of facts that would cause a well-grounded belief in the mind of a reasonable person. Such belief shall not be based on the fact that the check is of a particular class or is deposited by a particular class of persons. The reason for the bank's belief that the check is uncollectible shall be included in the notice required under paragraph (g) of this section.

(2)   *Overdraft and returned-check fees.* A depositary bank that extends the time when funds will be available for withdrawal as described in paragraph (e)(1) of this section, and does not furnish the depositor with written notice at the time of deposit shall not assess any fees for any subsequent overdrafts (including use of a line of credit) or return of checks or other debits to the account, if—

(i)   The overdraft or return of the check would not have occurred except for the fact that the deposited funds were delayed under paragraph (e)(1) of this section; and

(ii)   The deposited check was paid by the paying bank.

Notwithstanding the foregoing, the depositary bank may assess an overdraft or returned-check fee if it includes a notice concerning overdraft and returned-check fees with the notice of exception required in paragraph (g) of this section and, when required, refunds any such fees upon the request of the customer. The overdraft and returned-check notice must state that the customer may be entitled to a refund of overdraft or returned-check fees that are assessed if the check subject to the exception is paid and how to obtain a refund.

(f) *Emergency conditions.* Sections 229.11 and 229.12 do not apply to funds deposited by check in a depositary bank in the case of—

    (1) An interruption of communications or computer or other equipment facilities;

    (2) A suspension of payments by another bank;

    (3) A war; or

    (4) An emergency condition beyond the control of the depositary bank,

if the depositary bank exercises such diligence as the circumstances require.

(g) *Notice of exception.*

    (1) *In general.* When a depositary bank extends the time when funds will be available for withdrawal based on the application of an exception contained in paragraphs (b) through (f) of this section, it must provide the depositor with a written notice. The notice shall include the following information—

        (i) The account number of the deposit;

        (ii) The date and amount of the deposit;

        (iii) The amount of the deposit that is being delayed;

        (iv) The reason the exception was invoked; and

        (v) The day the funds will be available for withdrawal, unless the emergency conditions exception in paragraph (f) of this section has been invoked, and the depositary bank, in good faith, does not know the duration of the emergency and, consequently, when the funds must be made available at the time the notice must be given.

(2) *Timing of notice.*

    (i)   The notice shall be provided to the depositor at the time of the deposit, unless the deposit is not made in person to an employee of the depositary bank, or, if the facts upon which a determination to invoke one of the exceptions in paragraphs (b) through (f) of this section to delay a deposit only become known to the depositary bank after the time of the deposit. If the notice is not given at the time of the deposit, the depositary bank shall mail or deliver the notice to the customer as soon as practicable, but no later than the first business day following the day the facts become known to the depositary bank, or the deposit is made, whichever is later.

    (ii) If the availability of funds is delayed under the emergency-conditions exception provided in paragraph (f) of this section, the depositary bank is not required to provide a notice if the funds subject to the exception become available before the notice must be sent under paragraph (g)(2)(i) of this section.

(3) *Record retention.* A depositary bank shall retain a record, in accordance with section 229.21(g), of each notice provided pursuant to its application of the reasonable-cause exception under paragraph (e) of this section, together with a brief statement of the facts giving rise to the bank's reason to doubt the collectibility of the check.

(h) *Availability of deposits subject to exceptions.*

(1) If an exception contained in paragraphs (b) through (f) of this section applies, the depositary bank may extend the time periods established under sections 229.11 and 229.12 by a reasonable period of time.

(2) If a depositary bank invokes an exception under paragraph (e) of this section based on its reasonable cause to doubt collectibility of

a check that is subject to section 229.10(c)(1)(iii) or (v) or section 229.10(c)(2) to the extent that it applies to a check drawn on a Federal Reserve Bank or a Federal Home Loan Bank, or a cashier's, teller's, or certified check, the depository bank shall make the funds available for withdrawal not later than a reasonable period after the day the funds would have been required to be made available had the check been subject to section 229.11 or 229.12.

(3) If a depository bank invokes an exception under paragraph (f) of this section based on an emergency condition, the depository bank shall make the funds available for withdrawal not later than a reasonable period established in sections 229.11 and 229.12, whichever is later.

(4) For the purposes of paragraphs (h)(1),(2) and (3) of this section, an extension of up to four business days is a reasonable period. An extension of more than four business days may be reasonable, but the bank has the burden of so establishing.

SECTION 229.30—
Paying Bank's Responsibility for Return of Checks

(a) *Return of checks.* If a paying bank determines not to pay a check, it shall return the check in an expeditious manner as provided in either paragraph (a)(1) or (a)(2) of this section.

(1) *Two-day/four-day test.* A paying bank returns a check in an expeditious manner if it sends the returned check in a manner such that the check would normally be received by the depository bank not later than 4:00 p.m. (local time of the depository bank) of—

(i) The second business day following the banking day on which the check was presented to the paying bank, if the paying bank is located in the same check-processing region as the depository bank; or

(ii) The fourth business day following the banking day on which the check was presented to the paying bank, if the paying bank is not located in the same check-processing region as the depository bank.

If the last business day on which the paying bank may deliver a returned check to the depositary bank is not a banking day for the depositary bank, the paying bank meets the two-day/four-day test if the returned check is received by the depositary bank on or before the depositary bank's next banking day.

(2) *Forward collection test.* A paying bank also returns a check in an expeditious manner if it sends the returned check in a manner that a similarly situated bank would normally handle a check—

  (i) Of similar amount as the returned check;

  (ii) Drawn on the depositary bank; and

  (iii) Deposited for forward collection in the similarly situated bank by noon on the banking day following the banking day on which the check was presented to the paying bank.

Subject to the requirement for expeditious return, a paying bank may send a returned check to the depositary bank, or to any other bank agreeing to handle the returned check expeditiously under section 229.31(a). A paying bank may convert a check to a qualified returned check. A qualified returned check must be encoded in magnetic ink with the routing number of the depositary bank, the amount of the returned check, and a "2" in position 44 of the MICR line as a return identifier, in accordance with the American National Standard Specifications for Placement and Location of MICR Printing, X9.13 (Sept. 1983). This paragraph does not affect a paying bank's responsibility to return a check within the deadlines required by the UCC, Regulation J (12 CFR 210), or section 229.30(c).

(b) *Unidentifiable depositary bank.* A paying bank that is unable to identify the depositary bank with respect to a check may send the returned check to any bank that handled the check for forward collection even if that bank does not agree to handle the check expeditiously under section 229.31(a). A paying bank sending a returned check under this paragraph to a bank that handled the check for forward collection must advise the bank to which the check is sent that the paying bank is unable to identify the depositary bank. The expeditious-return requirements in section 229.30(a) do not apply to the paying bank's return of a check under this paragraph.

(c) *Extension of deadline for expedited delivery.* The deadline for return or notice of nonpayment under the UCC or Regulation J (12 CFR 210) is extended if a paying bank, in an effort to expedite delivery of a returned check to a bank, uses a means of delivery that would ordinarily result in the returned check's being received by the bank to which it is sent on or before the receiving bank's next banking day following the otherwise applicable deadline. The deadline is extended further if a paying bank uses a highly expeditious means of transportation, even if this means of transportation would ordinarily result in delivery after the receiving bank's next banking day.

(d) *Identification of returned check.* A paying bank returning a check shall clearly indicate on the face of the check that it is a returned check and the reason for the return.

(e) *Depositary bank without accounts.* The expeditious-return requirements of paragraph (a) of this section do not apply to checks deposited in a depositary bank that does not maintain accounts.

(f) *Notice in lieu of return.* If a check is unavailable for return, the paying bank may send in its place a copy of the front and back of the returned check, or, if no such copy is available, a written notice of nonpayment containing the information specified in section 229.33(b). The copy or notice shall clearly state that it constitutes a notice in lieu of return. A notice in lieu of return is considered a returned check subject to the expeditious-return requirements of this section and to the other requirements of this subpart.

(g) *Reliance on routing number.* A paying bank may return a returned check based on any routing number designating the depositary bank appearing on the returned check in the depositary bank's indorsement.

SECTION 229.31—
Returning Bank's Responsibility for Return of Checks

(a) *Return of checks.* A returning bank shall return a returned check in an expeditious manner as provided in either paragraph (a)(1) or (a)(2) of this section.

(1) *Two-day/four-day test.* A returning bank returns a check in an expeditious manner if it sends the check in a manner such that the check would normally be received by the depositary bank not later than 4:00 p.m. (local time) of—

    (i)   The second business day following the banking day on which the check was presented to the paying bank if the paying bank is located in the same check-processing region as the depositary bank; or

    (ii)   The fourth business day following the banking day on which the check was presented to the paying bank if the paying bank is not located in the same check-processing region as the depositary bank.

If the last business day on which the returning bank may deliver a returned check to the depositary bank is not a banking day for the depositary bank, the returning bank meets this requirement if the returned check is received by the depositary bank on or before the depositary bank's next banking day.

(2) *Forward collection test.* A returning bank also returns a check in an expeditious manner if it sends the returned check in a manner that a similarly situated bank would normally handle a check—

    (i)   Of similar amount as the returned check;

    (ii)   Drawn on the depositary bank; and

    (iii)   Received for forward collection by a similarly situated bank at the time the returning bank received the returned check, except that a returning bank may set a cut-off hour for the receipt of returned checks that is earlier than the similarly situated bank's cut-off hour for checks received for forward collection, if the cut-off hour is not earlier than 2:00 p.m.

Subject to the requirement for expeditious return, the returning bank may send a returned check to the depositary bank, or to any other bank agreeing to handle the returned check expeditiously under section 229.31(a). The returning bank may convert a check to a qualified returned check. A qualified returned check must be encoded in magnetic ink with the routing number of the depositary bank, the amount of the returned check, and a "2" in position 44 of the MICR line as a return identifier, in accordance with the American National Standard Specifications for Placement and Location of MICR Printing, X9.13 (Sept. 1983). The time for expeditious return under the forward-collection test, and the deadline for return under the UCC, Regulation J (12 CFR 210), are extended by one business day if the returning bank converts a returned check to a qualified returned check. This extension does not apply to the two-day/four-day test specified in paragraph (a)(1) of this section or when a returning bank is returning a check directly to the depositary bank.

(b) *Unidentifiable depositary bank.* A returning bank that is unable to identify the depositary bank with respect to a check may send the returned check to—

(1) Any collecting bank that handled the check for forward collection if the returning bank was not a collecting bank with respect to the returned check; or

(2) A prior collecting bank, if the returning bank was a collecting bank with respect to the returned check; even if that collecting bank does not agree to handle the check expeditiously under section 229.31(a). A returning bank sending a returned check under this paragraph must advise the bank to which the check is sent that the returning bank is unable to identify the depositary bank. The expeditious-return requirements in paragraph (a) of this section do not apply to return of a check under this paragraph. A returning bank that receives a returned check from a paying bank under section 229.30(a), but which is able to identify the depositary bank, must thereafter return the check expeditiously to the depositary bank.

(c) *Settlement.* A returning bank shall settle with a bank sending a returned check to it for return by the same means that it settles or could settle with the sending bank for a check received for forward collection drawn on the depositary bank. This settlement is final when made.

(d) *Charges.* A returning bank may impose a charge on a bank sending a returned check for handling the return.

(e) *Depositary bank without accounts.* The expeditious-return requirements of paragraph (a) of this section do not apply to checks deposited with a depositary bank that does not maintain accounts.

(f) *Notice in lieu of return.* If a check is unavailable for return, the returning bank may send in its place a copy of the front and back of the returned check, or, if no copy is available, a written notice of nonpayment containing the information specified in section 229.33(b). The copy or notice shall clearly state that it constitutes a notice in lieu of return. A notice in lieu of return is considered a returned check subject to the expeditious-return requirements of this section and to the other requirements of this subpart.

(g) *Reliance on routing number.* A returning bank may return a returned check based on any routing number designating the depositary bank appearing on the returned check in the depositary bank's indorsement or in magnetic ink on a qualified returned check.

SECTION 229.32—
Depositary Bank's Responsibility for Returned Checks

(a) *Acceptance of returned checks.* A depositary bank shall accept returned checks and written notices of nonpayment—

   (1) At a location at which presentment of checks for forward collection is requested by a depositary bank; and

   (2) (i) At a branch, head office, or other location consistent with the name and address of the bank in its indorsement on the check;

   (ii) If no address appears in the indorsement, at a branch or head office associated with the routing number of the bank in its indorsement on the check; or

   (iii) If no routing number or address appears in its indorsement on the check, at any branch or head office of the bank.

A depositary bank may require that returned checks be separated from forward collection checks.

(b) *Payment.* A depositary bank shall pay the returning or paying bank returning the check to it for the amount of the check prior to the close of business on the banking day on which it received the check ("payment date") by—

    (1) Debit to an account of the depositary bank on the books of the returning or paying bank;

    (2) Cash;

    (3) Wire transfer; or

    (4) Any other form of payment acceptable to the returning or paying bank;

    provided that the proceeds of the payment are available to the returning or paying bank in cash or by credit to an account of the returning or paying bank on or as of the payment date. If the payment date is not a banking day for the returning or paying bank or the depositary bank is unable to make the payment on the payment date, payment shall be made by the next day that is a banking day for the returning or paying bank. These payments are final when made.

(c) *Misrouted returned checks and written notices of payment.* If a bank receives a returned check or written notice of nonpayment on the basis that it is the depositary bank, and the bank determines that it is not the depositary bank with respect to the check or notice, it shall either promptly send the returned check or notice to the depositary bank directly or by means of a returning bank agreeing to handle the returned check expeditiously under section 229.31(a), or send the check or notice back to the bank from which it was received.

(d) *Charges.* A depositary bank may not impose a charge for accepting and paying checks being returned to it.

SECTION 229.33—Notice of Nonpayment

(a) *Requirement.* If a paying bank determines not to pay a check in the amount of $2,500 or more, it shall provide notice of nonpayment such that the notice is received by the depositary bank by 4:00 p.m. (local time) on the second business day following the banking day on which the check was presented to the paying bank. If the day the paying bank is required to provide notice is not a banking day for the depositary bank, receipt of notice on the depositary bank's next banking day constitutes timely notice. Notice may be provided by any reasonable means, including the returned check, a writing (including a copy of the check), telephone, Fedwire, telex, or other form of telegraph.

(b) *Content of notice.* Notice must include the—

(1) Name and routing number of the paying bank;

(2) Name of the payee(s);

(3) Amount;

(4) Date of the indorsement of the depositary bank;

(5) Account number of the customer(s) of the depositary bank;

(6) Branch name or number of the depositary bank from its indorsement;

(7) Trace number associated with the indorsement of the depositary bank; and

(8) Reason for nonpayment.

The notice may include other information from the check that may be useful in identifying the check being returned and the customers, and, in the case of a written notice, must include the name and routing number of the depositary bank from its indorsement. If the paying bank is not sure of an item of information, it shall include the information required by this paragraph to the extent possible, and identify any item of information for which the bank is not sure of the accuracy with question marks.

(c) *Acceptance of notice.* The depositary bank shall accept notices during its banking day—

(1) Either at the telephone or telegraph number of its return-check unit indicated in the indorsement, or, if no such number appears

in the indorsement or if the number is illegible, at the general-purpose telephone or telegraph number of its head office or the branch indicated in the indorsement, and

(2)   At any other number held out by the bank for receipt of notice of nonpayment, and, in the case of written notice, as specified in section 229.32(a).

(d)   *Notification of customer.* If the depositary bank receives a returned check or notice of nonpayment, it shall send notice to its customer of the facts by midnight of the banking day following the banking day on which it received the returned check or notice, or within a longer reasonable time.

(e)   *Depositary bank without accounts.* The requirements of this section do not apply to checks deposited in a depositary bank does not maintain accounts.

APPENDIX D

FEDERAL RESERVE RISK REDUCTION POLICY

THIRD PARTY ACCESS

DECEMBER 1990

FRRS
page 9-331 to 9-332

The Board has also adopted a proposal to allow arrangements whereby a depository institution or other entity ("the service provider") could initiate Fedwire transfers from the Federal Reserve account of another depository institution. Such arrangements will be permitted provided:

1. The institution whose account is being charged (the "institution") retains control of the credit-granting process by individually approving each transfer or establishing credit limits within which the service provider can act.

2. The service provider must be an affiliate of the institution, or, if the institution approves each individual transaction, an unaffiliated company. All service providers must be subject to examination.

3. The service provider must not permit or initiate transfers that would exceed individual customer credit limits without first obtaining the institution's permission.

4. The service provider must have the operational ability to ensure that the aggregate funds transfer activity of the institution does not result in daylight overdrafts in excess of the institution's cap.

195

5. All funds-transfer activity must be posted to the institution's account, and the institution will remain responsible for its account.

6. The institution's board of directors must approve the specifics of the arrangement, including (a) the operational transfer of the funds-transfer activity to the service provider, (b) the net debit cap for the activity to be processed by the service provider, and (c) the credit limits for any inter-affiliate funds transfers.

7. The institution and the service provider must execute an agreement with the relevant Reserve Banks delineating the terms of the agreement.

8. The institution must have adequate back-up procedures and facilities to cover equipment failure or other developments affecting the adequacy of the service being provided. This backup must provide the Reserve Bank with the ability to terminate a service-provider arrangement.

9. The institution must have the ability to monitor transactions being made on its behalf.

10. The institution must provide an opinion of counsel that the arrangement is consistent with corporate separateness and does not violate branching restrictions.

11. The primary supervisor must not object to the arrangement.

12. No individual with decision-making responsibilities relating to the funds-transfer area may hold such a position in more than one affiliated institution participating in an approved arrangement.

13. The institution must have in place an adequate audit program to review the arrangements at least annually to confirm that these arrangements are being met.

Any existing third-party arrangements that do not conform to these requirements should be phased out as soon as possible, but in no event later than June 30, 1990. In order to ensure consistency with the Board's policy, each new arrangement should be reviewed by the Directors of the Division of Federal Reserve Bank Operations prior to approval by the Reserve Bank.

INDEX

A

ACH credit origination, 32-48, 133-143
ACH credit funding, 85-86
ACH debit origination, 49-66
ACH debit funding, 86-87
ACH processor, 35, 50, 127, 131
ACH Risk Management Handbook, 9
Addenda records, 34
All electronic ACH, 9
American National Standards Institute (ANSI), 35
Approval process, 15-20
Article 4A, 162
Audit, 5, 160
Authentication, 69
Automated Clearing House, 6, 29, 31-69, 125, 130, 131,133-148
Automatic book transfer, 82-83
Availability schedule, 114, 131

B

Bank Administration Institute, 7-9
Banking Circular 235, 4, 7-8, 157, 161
Bankruptcy, 35, 51, 54, 70, 80, 81, 85, 98, 108, 122, 127, 135
Bearer securities, 122
Bilateral credit limits, 69
Board of directors, 6, 7, 157
Board of Trade Clearing Corporation, 8
Book-entry securities, 5, 8

C

Capital allocation, 139
Cash concentration, 10, 49, 54, 57-59, 63-66, 143-148
Cash letters, 79, 100, 102-104, 108, 116
Certificate of deposit, 121
Charitable contributions, 49
Check services, 6, 31, 79-116

Chicago Mercantile Exchange, 8
Clearing House Interbank Payments
    System (CHIPS), 8, 31, 162
Collateral, 38, 39, 42, 54, 55, 57, 59, 88,
    121, 132, 137, 142, 143, 146
Collectibility schedule, 114, 131
Consumer transactions, 34, 49-50
Controlled disbursement, 79, 81-95,
    127, 148-152
Corporate transactions, 34-35, 37, 50,
    107
Cost of capital, 129
Counterparty, 117, 122
Credit administration, 3, 13-24, 27,
    28, 39, 46, 47, 155
Credit approval, 54, 59, 77, 120
Credit file, 160
Credit grades, 14, 27, 39, 46, 59, 95,
    112
Credit limits, 7, 41-42, 73, 77, 120, 138,
    139
Credit policy, 16, 28, 161
Credit risk, 2, 13-15, 25-26, 35-36, 47,
    51, 69-70, 76-77, 80, 97, 100-103,
    105-107, 138, 160
Custody, 117, 123

D

Data collection vendor, 50, 146
Daylight overdraft, 2, 5, 30, 70, 73,
    119, 120, 129, 131, 132, 152
DDA system, 70
Delayed availability, 55, 57, 143, 145
Delivery versus payment, 10
Deposit concentration, 10, 49, 54, 57-
    59, 63-66, 143-148
Depository transfer check (DTC), 82,
    86-87, 98-99
Depository Trust Company, 8

Deteriorating credit, 18, 55, 57, 160
Direct debit, 49, 52-57, 59, 66, 126
Direct deposit of payroll, 15, 34, 36,
    37, 47, 49, 131, 141
Direct send, 104
Dividends, 34, 127
Downgrade, 47, 73, 135
Drawdown wire, 91
Duty officer, 30

E

EDIFACT, 35
Electronic Check Clearing House Or-
    ganization (Eccho), 107
Electronic data interchange (EDI), 31,
    34-35, 47, 130, 136, 153, 162
Electronic Funds Transfer Act
    (EFTA), 162
Encryption, 69

F

FDIC, 103
Federal Reserve, 4-7, 9, 35, 50, 51, 69,
    70, 76-77, 80, 91, 97, 105, 119, 121,
    129, 130, 131, 152
Fedwire, 8, 31, 69, 76
Fiduciary, 121, 122
Float, 79
Funds availability, 2, 55, 57, 143, 145
Funds control, 73, 119, 120, 132
Fraud, 3, 38, 41, 77, 138, 141, 142, 143

G

Government Securities Clearing
    Corporation (GSCC), 8
Group of Thirty, 7, 10, 125-126

Guarantees, 38, 39, 42, 54, 57, 59, 88, 121, 132, 137, 142, 143, 146

H

Health club payments, 49

I

Informal control, 25 -27, 157
Information gap, 82-83, 94
Insufficient balance, 4
Insurance, 141,147
Insurance premiums, 49
Interactive control, 25-26, 29-30, 32, 38-41, 57-59, 70, 73, 88-91, 114, 119-120, 129, 146
Intraday balance, 90, 91, 120
Intraday exposure, 82, 83, 94, 117, 121
Intraday line, 73-74, 90, 120, 139
Intraday overdraft, 91, 118
Irrevocable payment, 2, 4

L

Legal risk, 4
Legal agreement, 121
Lien, 121, 122
Liquidity, 4
Loan exposure, 140
Loan payments, 49
Lock box, 50, 103, 108-115
Loss funding, 132, 138-142, 147, 151

M

MICR line, 100
Mortgage payments, 49

N

NACHA payment formats, 35
NACHA Rules, 35, 50, 54, 126, 127
National Automated Clearing House Association (NACHA), 7, 9-10, 126
National Clearing House, 107
National Securities Clearing Corporation (NSCC), 8
Net debit cap, 5, 6, 69, 130
New customer approval, 17
New York Clearing House Association, 6, 69

O

Off balance sheet risk, 4
Office of the Comptroller of the Currency (OCC), 4, 157, 161
Options Clearing Corporation, 8
Operating limits, 41, 42
Operational risk, 2, 77, 138, 139, 141, 142, 143
Operations, 39, 46
Overlimit blocks, 30, 41, 42, 59, 138
Overnight overdraft, 83, 118
Over-the-counter deposits, 79, 103, 104

P

Participants Trust Company (PTC), 8
Password, 69
Payable through drafts, 79, 95-100
Payroll, 15, 34, 36, 37, 47, 49, 131, 141
Payments and Securities Systems Risk Project, 8

Periodic review, 15, 18, 25-28, 32, 39, 55-57, 59, 70-73, 88, 112-114, 119, 129, 146
Prefunding, 37-38, 39, 42, 47, 54, 133, 135, 136, 138, 142
Provisional funding, 100

R

Referral, 30, 42, 73, 120, 137, 138
Review process, 16-20
Receiving ACH credits, 49
Receiving ACH debits, 66
Receiver risk, 4
Regulation CC, 97, 105-106, 108, 114, 131, 143
Regulation E, 51, 126
Regulation J, 80
Reserve for credit losses, 141, 143, 151
Resolution Trust Corporation (RTC), 103
Retail lock box, 104
Retail securities services, 125
Return items, 2, 91, 105, 107, 108, 148, 150, 151
Right of recision, 51, 55, 65, 126
Risk control, 11, 30, 132, 137-138, 143, 146-147, 150-151, 156-157
Risk assessment, 5, 27, 121
Risk assessment guide, 8
Risk assessment worksheet, 42-47, 59-66, 74, 91-95, 100, 109-112
Risk-based capital, 5
Risk management plan, 47-48, 66, 74, 95, 100, 114-115, 121-122
Rolling settlement, 10

S

Safekeeping, 102-103, 117, 121, 123
Sales plans, 21
Securities, 6, 10, 117-128
Self-Assessment Guide, 6-7, 119, 130, 157
Sender risk, 4
Settlement, 4, 10
Software, 30, 41, 138
Social security, 49
Sovereign risk, 4
Sweep, 125
Systemic risk, 3, 4

T

Target balance, 85, 86, 90, 150
Task Force on Clearance and Settlement Reform in the U.S. Securities Markets, 126
Telephone bill paying, 34
Third party payroll processor, 15
Third party access, 7, 76-77
Third party ACH processor, 7
Third party data collection vendor, 50, 57
Thresholds for approval and review, 18, 20-24
Transit routing number, 82

U

Ungraded customers, 17, 18, 39, 46, 88, 158
Uniform Commercial Code, 162

V

Value added network, 34

W

Watch list, 17, 18, 42, 59, 94, 109, 112, 119, 135, 145, 150, 151, 158
Wholesale lock box, 103-104
Wire transfer, 29, 30, 31, 57, 59, 66, 69-76, 82, 83-85, 90, 91, 119, 130, 139, 143, 145-146

Z

Zero balance account, 81, 83, 150